The Hyena People

MW00827244

CONTRAVERSIONS

Critical Studies in Jewish Literature, Culture, and Society

Daniel Boyarin and Chana Kronfeld, General Editors

The Hyena People

Ethiopian Jews in Christian Ethiopia

Hagar Salamon

UNIVERSITY OF CALIFORNIA PRESS
Berkeley · Los Angeles · London

University of California Press
Berkeley and Los Angeles, California

University of California Press, Ltd.
London, England

© 1999 by the Regents of the University of
California

Library of Congress Cataloging-in-Publication Data

Salamon, Hagar.
  The hyena people : Ethiopian Jews in Christian
Ethiopia / Hagar Salamon.
       p.   cm.—(Contraversions ; 13)
  Includes bibliographical references and index.
  ISBN 0-520-21900-7 (alk. paper).—ISBN 0-520-
21901-5 (alk. paper)
    1. Jews—Ethiopia—Public opinion.
2. Animals—Mythology—Ethiopia.
3. Public opinion—Ethiopia.   4. Ethiopia—
Ethnic relations.   5. Jews, Ethiopian—Israel—
Interviews.   I. Title.   II. Series.
DS135.E75S26   1999
305.8924063—dc21   99-24291
                                                CIP

Manufactured in the United States of America
9 8 7 6 5 4 3 2 1

The paper used in this publication meets the
minimum requirements of ANSI/NISO Z39.48-
1992 (R 1997) (*Permanence of Paper*). ♾

Contents

Illustrations

Acknowledgments

For the writing of this book, the product of more than ten years of research and writing, I am hugely indebted.

It is impossible even to begin to thank the many scores of Ethiopian immigrants, now citizens of Israel, whose trust enabled them to open their hearts, their minds, and their homes to a struggling young scholar. I cannot expect to do full justice to their dignity, their honesty, and their openness. I can only hope that my occasional insensitivity and obtuseness did them no lasting harm. They honored me not only with their truth and certainties but also with their self-questioning. I hope this book gives some evidence that I learned from their example. Errors of omission and commission are, of course, exclusively my own.

This effort will always be associated in my mind with two towering Ethiopian figures. One of those is Dejen (Gideon) Mengesha, for whom no ignorance of mine was impenetrable. I deeply regret that his premature death prevented him from sharing the published results of his illuminations. For *qes* Avraham, the Beta Israel priest who became a close friend and advisor during my research, I have inexpressible affection and veneration.

An unredeemable debt is owed to Professor Harvey Goldberg, the mentor who has guided me in anthropology from my undergraduate days to the present. His gentle, quiet, unintrusive persistence taught me about the relationship between manifest personal regard and scholarly proficiency. His gift for listening helped me to discover my own voice. To Professor Galit Hasan-Rokem, who never sacrificed her concern for the person inside the subject and whose mastery of many scholarly fields was a constant wonder and inspiration, I owe my thanks for help in forming my own synthesis. Professor Steven Kaplan's deep understanding of Ethiopian history and culture aided me in the deciphering of what otherwise might have been an unintelligible codex. His intellectual courage and support were a constant goad and challenge.

I am grateful to colleagues who worked their way through the developing manuscript: Professor Eyal Ben-Ari, Professor Erik Cohen, and Professor Don Handelman. For intellectual stimulation and good advice I thank Professor Alan Dundes, Dr. Heda Jason, and Professor Richard Pankhurst. Professor Daniel Boyarin contributed his inspiring suggestion concerning the title of the book and much more. Douglas A. Arava of the University of California Press provided valuable advice and enthusiastic support. Professor Olga Kapeliuk and Anbessa Teferra painstakingly guided me through the subtleties of Ethiopian dialects and Amharic transcription, for which I thank them deeply. The four referees of the book, each of whom reviewed the manuscript from a unique vantage point, offered excellent suggestions which contributed significantly to the final shape of the book.

My sincere gratitude goes to Richard Korn for fine-tuning the English translation and to Jessie Bonn, Azzan Meir-Levi and Sara Friedman for their editorial support and criticism. Nathan Dror and Judy Goldberg were both important for their wisdom and reassurance at crucial moments.

The following foundations generously supported me through all stages of this work: The Shaine Center for Research in the Social Sciences; The Center for Integration of Oriental Jewish Heritage at the Ministry of Education; The JDC, Jerusalem; The Sephardic Community Committee; The Fulbright Fellowship for Post-Doctoral Studies; The Hebrew University Grant for Post-Doctoral Studies; The Lucius M. Littauer Foundation; The Mexican Friends of the Hebrew University (Women's Section); The Harry S. Truman Research Institute for the Advancement of Peace. To the individuals who staff those fine organizations, I should like to extend my most personal regards.

My family gave unfailing support. My mother Miriam, whose critical tact enabled me to risk uttering my most random, half-formed thoughts, shared a deep companionship. I could not have completed this ten-year work without the distracting interference of my four daughters, Mika, Noga, Zohar, and Netta. Their sheer presence was a constant incentive whose joyfulness more than compensated for the preoccupations of mothering. To their father, Amos, who has been my companion through the drama of all five deliveries, I dedicate this book.

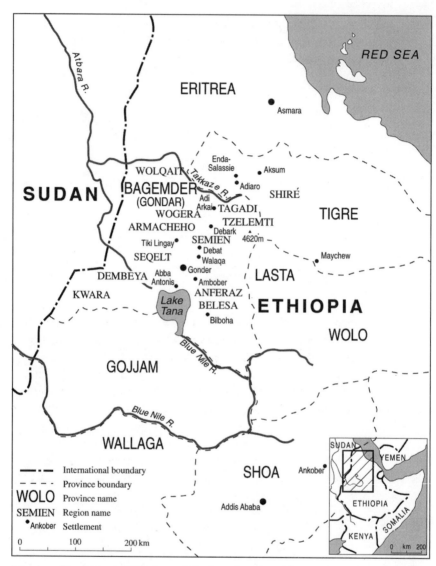

Map 1. Provinces and Regions of the Beta Israel in Ethiopia

¥Introduction

A particular event constantly resurfaces in my mind, demanding to be told and giving form to the entire quest that led to this book. It was *qes* Avraham, the Jewish priest from Tigre in northern Ethiopia, who approached me with a request, many months after we became acquainted and following long hours during which I listened to his reminiscences: "I'm told that there are Christian Ethiopians living in Jerusalem. You live in Jerusalem, you know where they are, I need to talk to them. I implore you, take me to see them." I agreed. On a broiling August day, I picked him up from the Jerusalem Rabbinical Institute, where he was studying, far from his desert hometown in the south of Israel. With his dark Western-style suit and light-colored shirt, *qes* Avraham seemed more youthful from one meeting to the next. He is of slight build with bronze features and dark shining eyes; an enigmatic smile plays over his face when he recounts especially painful memories.

When we entered Ethiopia Street, I couldn't help but think of the special mythological ties between Jerusalem and Ethiopia, starting with the fabled meeting between King Solomon and the Queen of Sheba. After a short walk in the narrow alley, between two looming stone walls, the majestic Ethiopian Church suddenly appeared. The church's round courtyard, built of local stone, provided a shady refuge from the teeming city that lay just beyond the heavy metal gate. The clergy, several of whom have lived in Jerusalem for decades, reside in the low, narrow monastic cells along the courtyard's inner walls. The rooms face the massive, impressive church situated in the center of the courtyard. Ethiopian priests, monks, and nuns in long dark robes cross the courtyard with silent steps. *Qes* Avraham entered the compound, introduced himself to the priests as a Jewish *qes*,[1] then straight-away drew them into conversation.

Within a short time, *qes* Avraham and Abba Abram of the church were absorbed in a lively discussion. I sat watching these men of two different Ethiopian religions discussing theological matters in a church in Jerusalem. *Qes* Avraham was extremely intense. He argued that the Jews' arrival in Jerusalem was incontrovertible proof that, despite the superiority of the Christians in Ethiopia, God favors the Jews. I was struck by the sense of urgency with which my friend approached the standing of the Christians and by his consuming need to have the last word in an argument which had obvious never left his thoughts, even years after he had left Ethiopia.

Qes Avraham and I had traversed a long road together in our mutual endeavor to breathe life into his past in Ethiopia, leading up to this theological discussion in the heart of Jerusalem. My first encounter with Jews from Ethiopia had taken place more than twelve years before, a few months prior to my meeting with *qes* Avraham. Even today I savor the astonishment I first experienced when I saw the knots of dark-skinned people grouped near my house, the men wearing knitted *kipot,* the women in gleaming white robes embroidered down the entire length in black, red, yellow, and green. To my even greater amazement, I saw among the tattoos on their bodies the symbol of the cross.

They seemed to materialize from nowhere, coming in large, organized groups to visit the Western Wall near my home. Operation Moses was under way: one of the two clandestine operations in which the Beta Israel (Falasha)[2]—about 50,000 members—were brought from Ethiopia to Israel.[3]

My own personal quest began in 1984. During Operation Moses, I accepted an offer to participate in fieldwork conducted by the Ministry of Absorption in order to evaluate the integration of Ethiopian immigrants in Israel. The work required me to visit absorption centers throughout Israel and observe and interview the staff. At the time, a wave of enthusiasm colored by a warm, all-embracing paternalism washed over the country. I would pass through the crowded central bus stations of Jerusalem and Tel Aviv and on to smaller towns, until finally I reached the absorption center I was to visit on that day. It might be a hotel that had been converted into housing for entire families from Ethiopia. They were put in rooms painted pink, with open closets, a wide bed, and wall-to-wall carpeting. When not studying Hebrew, the inhabitants passed the time in the hotel corridors or lobby. Groups of children expertly rode the elevator; it became their most exciting game. At other times, I might arrive at an as yet uninhabited neighborhood which served as an absorption center. From the outside it appeared no different from many other standard housing projects in Israel, but it was immediately clear that a single, homogeneous group occupied it. Usually, however, the typical center was a caravan (mobile home) site thrown up especially to house the tide of immigrants from Ethiopia. On a bare, rectangular plot of land, light-colored caravans were set a few meters apart, divided into several housing units. A few steps, on which the inhabitants whiled away long hours, led to cement paths connecting the tiny apartments. The long days that I spent at the caravan sites gave me a sense of desolation. Like grains of coarse salt scattered on bare ground, where nothing but brambles grew, the caravans appeared as dreary islands.

I would arrive at one of the absorption centers, always after a long ride on several buses. The Absorption Ministry assumed that the way to pinpoint the difficulties in the absorption process was to speak to the officials. So I had to approach the staff: the Hebrew teachers, social workers, and Ethiopian interpreters. Very rarely did I have a chance to conduct stammered conversations with the immigrants themselves, who would usually wait outside the office, or sit in the classes I visited, or eat next to me in the hotel dining room. Although I had daily contact with them, the members of the community remained a sealed-off entity for me, becoming more and more monolithic and uniform, as they were refracted through the reports of the absorption center staff. Only gradually, in the course of the several months that I was engaged in the project, did I become aware, with growing turmoil, that this group challenged existing definitions of Jewish and Israeli identity.

At the time I couldn't put my finger on the exact reason for this, but I could not shake off the shock of the first sight of them. The crosses tattooed on their hands and foreheads remained a vivid symbol for me, shattering long-standing perceptions of Jewish identity. After the completion of the Absorption Ministry project, I returned to those same absorption centers, but this time I quickly bypassed the offices—with the secret, almost guilty sense of tasting forbidden fruit—and went straight to the apartments of the immigrants themselves. I wanted to invite their past to enter our dialogues through the special lens of their individual memories and to explore with them the all-important question that occupied me: *Who was a Jew in Ethiopia?*

This question sparked in turn a myriad of equally perplexing issues: What was the essence of the dividing line between Jews and their non-Jewish neighbors? How did they portray their daily lives in Ethiopia as perceived through distances of time and place? How did they view themselves within the interreligious dynamics that they experienced in Ethiopia?

Although these issues were formulated in a manner that might indicate the existence of a fixed answer lying "out there" waiting to be unveiled, identity is in fact far more elusive, shaped and reshaped in memory, and expressed in different forms and contexts. The constant process of identity formation accelerates dramatically with the passage of identity in Israel, from Jews in black Ethiopia to blacks in Jewish Israel. Within this state of flux, however, as this book attempts to illustrate, transactions of the present are mediated through deeper constructs with which the present engages in an ongoing dialogue. Memory as dialogue is fundamental to this entire process. Its precise formulation was the preoccupation of my encounters with the people I interviewed. The Ethiopia located in Beta Israel memory was the ethnographic landscape I was struggling to capture.[4] My quest was for the Ethiopia within them.

Back in their native Ethiopia, the Beta Israel constituted a religious and professional minority scattered across the vast reaches of northwestern Ethiopia amid a predominantly Christian population with whom they shared both physical appearance and language. According to studies on the origins of the Beta Israel, the group originated from an apostatic movement that broke off from Ethiopian Christianity in the fifteenth century.[5] While the question of the group's actual origins is pertinent to the question of their Jewish lineage, their self-identity as Jews in Ethiopia was defined, more than anything else, vis-à-vis the Christian "other." The Beta Israel regarded themselves as a distinct religious group upholding a religion forsaken by the majority for the younger, now dominant religion of Christianity. Their faith clustered around the *Orit*, the Old Testament written in Ge'ez, the language of both Jewish and Christian sacred writings. As a group, the Beta Israel strongly identified with the *Orit*[6] and constructed their identity in reference to their Christian neighbors, rather than to a Jewish "other." This situation did not change significantly until recent decades, when the awareness of a Jewish meaningful "other" became more fully present in the Beta Israel consciousness. The enigma of Jewish life in Ethiopia and the dramatic airlift of almost the entire community to the State of Israel aroused public debate both within the Jewish world and without. Implicitly assuming a dichotomous separation between Jews and non-Jews, the sole aim of these debates was a clear-cut answer to the question: Are the Falasha "real" Jews? Previous studies dealing with this group had been occupied with the same question. The question persists. One school of thought characterizes their lives in terms of isolation from their surroundings and ongoing struggles and emphasizes their similarity to other—primarily historical—Jewish groups.[7] A second school focuses on the cultural and religious similarities between them and their Ethiopian neighbors.[8] Without diminishing the inherent interest in the debate between these polar approaches, I find the explanations engendered by both views to be riddled with contradictions and ambiguity.

The ethnographic study of cultural relations in Ethiopia at the level of daily interaction as recalled by Beta Israel is as important as the prevailing historical approach. Accordingly, I will concentrate on exploring concepts and dynamics that molded the intercommunal relations and were in turn molded by them. While most research in this field hitherto has dealt with the *consequences* of the encounter between Beta Israel and their neighbors, I am interested in the *experience* of the encounter itself. This experience is positioned, albeit tenuously, in the group's memory and in the consciousness they brought with them to Israel. Incidents such as the mesmerizing meeting between *qes* Avraham and the Christian clergy of the Ethiopian church in Jerusalem led me to question whether either model offered an adequate framework for understanding the life of the Jews in Christian Ethiopia. As I pursued this inquiry, it became increasingly apparent that for Ethiopian Jews, relations with Christians are not something which they left behind but are an expression of a fundamental aspect of their very identity, an identity inextricably pervaded by intergroup dynamics. The Jewish–Christian rubric cannot be overemphasized, for the Jews defined themselves and their activities largely in relation to the dominant Christian society. The ethnography of Jewish life in Ethiopia *is* the ethnography of the Jews' relations with their Christian neighbors.[9]

At the same time there is a constant, ongoing dialectic defining their identity as a separate group within this Ethiopian Christian world. There is, then, an affinity between the "external" scholarly models, on one hand, and the complex and multifaceted conceptual system and ideology of Beta Israel themselves, on the other. An understanding of the life of this group,

including its contemporary self-narration, must be sensitive to the
Ethiopian cultural characteristics shared by the Beta Israel. It should also
reflect the particular responses that Beta Israel developed to that culture,
especially to its Christian elements. This book is, in many ways, an
ethnography of the fantasies and fears, the facts and fictions, that divided
groups and in particular Jews and non-Jews. Beta Israel brought with
them to Israel an ongoing internal dialectic defining their identity as a
separate entity. Beta Israel memories comprise the cultural and historical imagination of a people redefining their own sense of place in history. The specific contents are constantly redefined in light of changing
reality, but on many levels of consciousness, the conceptual frame of reference remains meaningful in the new cultural context in Israel.

When I first made the acquaintance of *qes* Avraham, his search for a
bridge between the past in Ethiopia and the present in Israel eventually
led him to the Old City of Jerusalem. Our meetings there followed a fixed
ritual. I would pick him up at the last stop on the bus route that ran from
the new neighborhood where he lived, through Jerusalem's main street,
and ended at Jaffa Gate, the main gate in the Old City walls. After he
got off the bus, we would greet each other with a smile and steer our
way through the steep, colorful winding alleys of the market toward the
Western Wall. We would tarry there for a moment, then climb the pre-
cipitous stairs until we stood in the doorway of my nearby small apartment in the Jewish quarter of the Old City. We would sit across the
kitchen table and discuss Ethiopia, Israel, and whatever lay in between.
Gradually, the conversations departed from the predictable formula in
which his every reply was a monologue recounting the yearnings of the
Jews for Jerusalem and their rigorous observance of Judaism over thou-
sands of years. He began to recount personal anecdotes, filled with
minutely detailed descriptions, thoughts, and feelings.

As early as my initial conversations with *qes* Avraham, it became clear
to me that when he spoke of Jews, he was speaking of Christians as well,
though Beta Israel also lived among a mixed population of Muslims and
others.[10] Even in areas highly populated with Muslims, it was still the
Christians who dominated the life of the Jews. The mere presence of the
Muslims, as preserved in the memory of the informants, lent a resonance
to the drama being played out before them. The stories I heard were a
narrative reenactment of the Oedipal conflict between Judaism and
Christianity—religion born of religion, and, in the ironic inversions of
daily interaction, religion dominated by religion—that was acted out so

powerfully in Ethiopia. The clarification of this drama became a personal challenge for me.

The stark contrast between the landscape where the interviews were conducted—the bleak absorption centers—and the landscape evoked by their memories, brimming with sensuality, was a source of challenge and tension.[11] Was it at all possible to "recreate" their Ethiopia in the dreary rooms of the absorption centers, so foreign to their native landscape? Now that they themselves were no longer there, was it possible to approach any closer the riddle of Jewish life in Ethiopia?

Grounded in the understanding that ethnography is a scholarly construction of interpretations[12]—both the group's and my own—this book grew out of more than a hundred in-depth interviews with members of the group who immigrated to Israel from different regions in Ethiopia. Taking its data from participants' multifaceted accounts, impressions, and interpretations of their daily lives, the study seeks to rise from the descriptive to the analytic. Recurring patterns of structure and content suggested that anthropological exploration might provide tools for understanding the contingent relations between a variety of themes which on the surface seemed unrelated, including religious disputations, notions of purity and impurity, the concept of blood, slavery and conversion, supernatural powers, the transmutation of natural elements, the metaphors of clay vessels, water, and fire, and the image of the Ethiopian Jew as a hyena. These themes comprise a conceptual system which stands for a reality often perceived by the Jews as baffling and incoherent.

A significant example: the Jews in Ethiopia owned no land but worked as tenant farmers on Christian land.[13] No less central was their work as craftsmen, the men specializing in smithery and the women in pottery. Local Christian society treated these crafts with ambivalence. Though derided, and their practitioners despised, these products were not only essential to that agricultural society but also highly valued for their quality. This ambivalence was expressed by attributing supernatural powers to the artisans, to account for the extraordinary quality of their products. The Jew was depicted as *buda,* hyena-man, a supernatural being who crosses the line between the human and the inhuman. Although this figure appears frequently in African folklore in general and in the literature dealing with other minority groups in Ethiopia, face-to-face accounts conveyed much more than any writing can. The people sharing their memories with me testified that they had been perceived by their Christian neighbors as hyenas who disguised themselves as humans during the day, only to assume their animal form again at night.

Unprepared for what followed from this uncanny, utterly strange rev-elation, and alarmed by all the possible pitfalls in our face-to-face inter-view dialogue, I caught my breath. I was afraid my reactions would be-tray me. Bit by bit I learned to integrate these deeply mythical layers of information into the context of the world picture that was gradually re-vealed to me by my partners in dialogue. I learned to accept the charged experiences—many more of which would surface later—in the same matter-of-fact spirit in which they were presented to me.

Some striking instances of attitudes presented as contradictory by the Beta Israel: the Christians linked their Jewish neighbors to the *buda* im-age through a series of accusations which indicted them while profiting from them. These accusations, invariably tinged with religion, encom-passed their crafts, their unlanded status, and their Judaism. Thus, the Jewish smith was regarded as a direct descendant of the Jew who forged the nails for Jesus' crucifixion. Yet, these same Christians often show-ered Jewish religious leaders with requests for prayers in times of trou-ble. Ambivalence toward the Jews was further expressed in efforts at con-version, which often bore fruit. The Jews perceived these efforts as a sign of the esteem in which they were held by the Christians. Additional signs of recognition were the Christians' high regard for the Old Testament and its adherents. Thus the Jews of Ethiopia often found relations with their Christian neighbors incoherent and confusing.

What baffled my interviewees also baffled me. Was there a dominant organizing principle that might make sense of what confused us all? Ac-cusations of sorcery and magic provided the first clues. The kindly Jew-ish blacksmith who forged your scythe might well turn out to be the hyena who dug up your family funeral plot last night. In a world governed by the supernatural, seemingly innocent things and people could suddenly turn on you by turning themselves into something else.

The unifying concept was *malevolent transformation:* the ability at-tributed to the Jews to assume a different shape, mostly with evil intent, transform the physical form of actual objects, and even cause them to change their nature. As a central idiom, this dynamic affected the most fundamental concerns of human life, shaping ideas, images, and precepts, and was also strikingly evident in the passage from one mode of expres-sion to another. My interviewees thus frequently switched between modes of expression, be they descriptions of everyday life, rituals, mythological stories, or proverbs. These transitions were accompanied by changing moods, facial expressions, tone of voice, and gestures. I was made aware of the centrality of this process as I apprehended striking changes in moods and modes of expression, which constitute the meta-messages of communication. This master principle paved the way for a fuller understanding of the group's existence in Ethiopia.

The journey described in the book began in the cramped confines of the absorption centers and housing projects where the Ethiopian Jews live in Israel. We would usually sit in the family living room, considered the most respectable place in the apartment. During my five years of fieldwork, these rooms accumulated furniture and electrical appliances, bought for the most part with the aid of the absorption grant and considered by the immigrants to be symbols of Western culture. Although I wandered among settlements of immigrants from the north of Israel to the south, the rooms where we discussed life in Ethiopia were exact replicas of each other, and the almost total identity between them communicated to me the inhabitants' sense of insecurity. Following some preordained sequence, a sophisticated television set was bought, then a velvet-upholstered couch, love seat, and armchair set placed around a coffee table. The items of furniture were always distributed in the room in the same order. Before much time elapsed, a shiny new breakfront was set up opposite the couch. This piece of furniture became a ceremonial focus when the television and video were installed there, amid sets of Western crockery. Only much later, almost stealthily, did they begin to display Ethiopian straw trays wound with colored wool, which the Ethiopian women wove in Israel, photographs of relatives, posters from the Ethiopian airlines company, and Ethiopian maps patterned in yellow, green, and red, the colors of the Ethiopian flag.

From the moment of their arrival in Israel, the immigrants were exposed to invasive interference in their intimate, private lives. Absorption officials, whom they called *feranj*, the Ethiopian appellation for whites, usually female, entered their homes, their kitchens, and even more intimate corners of their new living areas. Acknowledging that academic study is also a kind of appropriation by the Israeli establishment, I thought it would be wise to create as clear-cut a distinction as possible between myself and these officials, especially between the interactions characterizing the two different types of meetings. I struggled to achieve the status of a guest, invited to their home in order to learn from them, not to teach them. Our meetings would usually commence with a long drawn-out silence. Following repeated greetings and salutations, I would usually initiate the conversation. "Life here is not like life in Ethiopia," I suggested. "I've never been there and it's very hard to find books telling

Figure 1.   Sitting with neighbors, Walaqa, Ethiopia, 1984. Photograph by
Doron Bacher, courtesy of Beth Hatefutsoth Photo Archive.

how things were for you in Ethiopia," I added. "I've come to you to learn
about your life there."

Usually silence would resume as soon as I finished speaking. I would
start again: "Life in Ethiopia—your homes, the synagogues, your
neighbors—you left it all behind. Even if you could go visit the villages
now that you're here, we can't tell how life was when you lived there.
There must also be differences from one region to the other. Ethiopia is
much larger than Israel, and the Jews were scattered among many villages. That's why I have to ask people what they remember."

Our journey was a linking of fragmented situations, each with a separate beginning, middle, and end. It became no easier for me to present
my request each time anew as the quest advanced, but other difficulties
contributed to my sense of standing on shaky ground. I would often arrive for an interview after an exhausting bus ride, only to find that the
person I had come to see had suddenly left to visit relatives, or attend a
wedding or a memorial service. The rhetoric of the interview reflected
the flux of change and inquiry throughout all the long years of research.
It was not a search for the flying carpet that would transport me to
Ethiopia in the period when Jews lived there but a quest for the means
to lead me to the Ethiopia that they harbored within.

I discovered, however, yet another Ethiopia that emerged in the

Figure 2. Villagers, Ethiopia, 1984. Photograph by G. Sabar-Freidman.

Figure 3. Preparing food in the village, Ethiopia. Photograph by G. Sabar-Freidman.

process of reminiscing. This was the Ethiopia that assumed an increasingly important status in intra-group discussions and was also reflected in material culture, in music and videos, and in the decorations adorning their new Israeli apartments. This Ethiopia reflected the transition in identity from Jews in black Ethiopia to Ethiopians in Jewish Israel. Characteristic of *this* Ethiopia was the fact that it collapsed individual stories, creating a more iconic, almost monolithic Ethiopian entity.

I developed techniques which would repersonalize the Ethiopia within my partners in dialogue and encourage the flow of memories. Thus, for instance, meeting an interviewee for the first time, I would refer to a map of Ethiopia that I carried with me. The map enabled us to attain a certain distance from the investigative context and drew us closer to Ethiopia. Poring together over the piece of paper that epitomized the "other place" rendered the discussion more serious and tangible for the interviewees. I encouraged the interviewees to begin with a general physical description of their village and its inhabitants. I asked them to tell me of daily activities and social encounters, to explain and interpret them for me by whatever means they chose. In addition to such verbal discourse, I drifted into random activities such as clearing the cups on the table or leafing through a booklet I would find in the room. I even came to the last interviews with my eldest daughter, who was then a baby, changing her diaper or feeding her precisely when the topics of discussion were complex and especially sensitive, for instance, magical accusations or slavery.

To this day I don't know whether these conscious and half-conscious attempts had any impact at all on the progress of the interview. The fact that they occurred simultaneously with the most open, in-depth, and flexible interviews underlines, in my opinion, more than anything else, my own need for security and perhaps even control, albeit minor and temporary, of the dialogue situation.

Most of the interviews were initiated by myself, in a structured framework arranged and agreed upon by both parties. In the many meetings, I usually sat in the informant's apartment, facing a single interviewee, totally absorbed by his or her descriptions and explanations. At times other people were present at the interview, mainly family, neighbors, or relatives. These conversations had their own dynamics, marked by the interplay between the different partners to dialogue as they spoke to each other on different subjects. Throughout this quest there ran a strong tension between two simultaneous currents: the past life in Ethiopia and the present life in Israel. The fieldwork engaged both. The controversy regarding the immigrants' Jewish status probably raised questions in their minds about whether the interview could aid or harm them. Obviously, I could not assume that it was only the past they were recounting to me; their narration was certainly colored by the present. Often the interviewees traveled back emotionally to their villages in Ethiopia. Thus, for instance, although interviews were conducted in Hebrew, the interviewees as a matter of course used the Ethiopian derogatory terms leveled at them by their neighbors. On other occasions, their descriptions were accompanied by emotional outbursts, verbal reenactments of daily scenes, and so forth. However, they also incorporated into their accounts expressions taken from the Israeli context to facilitate communication between us. For example, the title *rabbi* was used instead of *qes*. Examples taken from Jewish–Arab relations in Israel or referring to distances between different places in Israel served to concretize relationships and distances in Ethiopia. This dialogical tactic can be understood on two levels, with the connection between them highly complex. On one level, it indicates the difficulty of "translating" terms as they pass from one culture to another. On another, the discourse took place in two modes of expression: one in Hebrew, in an apartment in Israel, with a white Israeli woman who typified the immediate context; and then the more profound level of a psychological return to Ethiopia. The interviewees represented different points on the continuum stretching between the two levels, the immediate (Israeli) and the deeper (Ethiopian) that I have noted. Put schematically, the more adept and practiced the interviewee was at presenting the life of the group in Ethiopia to an external audience, the more heightened his awareness of the immediacy of the interview situation.

Such interviews frequently opened with escapist descriptions like those recounted by *qes* Avraham, a kind of attempt to depart from the framework of the dialogic interview and pass into a formulaic defensive narration, though even in this type of interview certain important issues were addressed for the first time. The conversation about these issues was marked by a more "direct" sense of return to Ethiopia. The nonverbal messages I drew upon, which I judged to be most efficient in releasing tension, contributed to diverting the interview from the immediate present to the "other place." Most of the people I spoke with had not previously been interviewed about their lives in Ethiopia, and most still lived in the isolation of the Ethiopian communities in Israel. Thus, for instance, in three cities in the south of Israel where I conducted fieldwork, the interviewees lived in Western-style apartment buildings, in a neighborhood with other

Ethiopian immigrants living in identical apartments, and they would pass from one apartment to the other visiting each other, as if it were a single, virtually self-contained space. These circumstances, with all their implications, heightened the sense of the "return" to Ethiopia in the interviews.

In addition to these lengthy, in-depth interviews, which lasted between two and five hours and often stretched over more than one session, I had spontaneous informal interviews, usually of shorter duration. Sometimes the most acute issues would emerge precisely in these circumstances, apparently due to the unforeseen, less constraining nature of these meetings.

A gap of several years lies between the immediate time of the interview and the time it evokes, a gap during which the group underwent far-reaching transformations. The transformations produced by this passage of time are indicated by the fact that communication in the interviews was carried out in Hebrew peppered with Ethiopian expressions and terms. The language shift thus stood for a whole other set of changes, transformations, and shifts in perspective in the search for the territories of memory.

The flow of time addressed by the study was comprised, then, of the two levels simultaneously. On the immediate level, "time" was the Past. The interview was conducted in a new context, a new language, evoking a reality that had disappeared. In some way the interview was an attempt to reconstruct it verbally. But the prime interest of the present work is with the conceptual system and its different levels of cultural manifestation: on a deeper level, the "time" of the study was the "continuing present," which was no longer a part of their daily reality but powerfully structured the dialogue between them and Israeli society. There were additional nuances. Thus, for instance, while deep in fieldwork I got married. I invited qes Avraham and his wife to the small ceremony. Festive in a Western-style suit, his wife Yaffa wearing a flowing white Ethiopian robe, they arrived by bus with their small son from the city in the south where they lived. The gift they brought was surprising, moving, and thought-provoking, especially as it did not match my cultural expectations. It comprised three elements: a Western porcelain coffee-and-cake set; a typical Ethiopian straw tray woven by qes Avraham's wife in Israel; and a sizable sum of money that he stuck into my husband's shirt pocket, mumbling awkwardly, "This is how we give." I was extremely moved by the immense effort and expense qes Avraham put into the three wedding presents. I sensed that there was an important message hidden in these gifts, but I lacked the appropriate tools to grasp it. Another year of fieldwork went by, and descriptions of wedding presents offered by Jews to their Christian neighbors accumulated on my tape recorder. While

Figure 4.   Roasting coffee beans, Ethiopia. Photograph by
G. Sabar-Freidman.

still trying to decipher their meaning, I suddenly became aware of some
hidden messages expressed by the wedding gifts. While clearly echoing
the traditional gift-giving usages with which *qes* Avraham was familiar
in Ethiopia, it also seemed to reflect the new, complex system of identi-
ties he had assumed in Israel. This research has been an attempt to capture a consciousness by means of communication—something both rec-
ognizable in its universal human quality, yet utterly mysterious—in its
foreign, intimate, and sacred specificity.

CHAPTER 1

Insults and Ciphers

The Vocabulary of Denigration

Small round huts of wood, straw, and mud, which can be erected in a few short days, fill the tiny villages scattered along the steep mountains and broad plains of northwestern Ethiopia. These are the scenes to which the Beta Israel, the Jews of Ethiopia, return time and again in their memories. In their thoughts they experience the spaces in an intimate fashion, as though a part of their own bodies. Time and again they speak the names of their villages, describe the distances between them, and make the mental journey along the paths leading from one village to another. They carry with them a precise "map" of the villages in their home region—though they never used a map in Ethiopia—and a powerful yearning, an almost physical ache, for the animals, particularly the cows, they left behind when they came to Israel.

The Beta Israel lived in more than 500 small villages concentrated, for the most part, in the regions close to Lake Tana and north of it in the Tigre, Gondar, and Wolo regions of Ethiopia.[1] In a few of the villages the population was made up exclusively of Beta Israel, but in most cases the Jews lived in villages which were predominantly Christian, Muslim, or—in a few instances—polytheist. They lived close to their Christian neighbors, spoke the same language, and shared the same physical traits. Yet despite these similarities, the group's current—albeit evolving—corpus of tradition[2] characterizes them as a distinct group: Jews who had come to Ethiopia from Israel in ancient times and had valiantly preserved their faith throughout the centuries. They worked primarily in agriculture,

Figure 5.   Weaver in front of his hut, Ethiopia. Photograph by G. Sabar-Freidman.

tenants on plots of land that belonged to Christians. As mentioned in the Introduction, they also specialized in specific crafts—smithery the men, pottery the women. Both crafts employ fire, and thus the sight of thick black smoke became a sign of Jewish presence in a given village.

The Beta Israel maintained their own special sites within the village: *masgid, bet-qeddus,* or *bet-tselot,* a house of prayer whose name varied by region; *yedem gojo* (blood hut), *yedem bet* (house of blood), or *ya-margam gojo* (hut of the curse), situated at the periphery of the residential huts,[3] where Jewish women would sit, separated, during their menstrual and postpartum periods; and just outside the village, the Jewish cemetery known as *qaber bet* (house of burial). When the Jews recall their villages in Ethiopia, they speak of the daily routine, of the neighbors with whom they lived in such close proximity, and of what set them apart from these same neighbors.

A complex system of daily contact existed between the Jews and their Christian neighbors: a framework of formalities of attraction and repulsion which permitted structured cooperation but at the same time set strict boundaries between the groups. These were most clearly evident in the prohibition against physical contact. For the Jews, physical contact with any person who was not one of the Beta Israel (and was thus considered impure) was prohibited. According to official rhetoric, when

Figure 6. People in their village, Ethiopia, 1984. Photograph by G. Sabar-Freidman.

Figure 7. Jewish woman grinding wheat, Walaqa, Ethiopia, 1984. Photograph by Doron Bacher, courtesy of Beth Hatefutsoth Photo Archive.

even the slightest contact occurred either accidentally or due to some necessity, contamination resulted and the Jew was expected to undergo ritual purification.[4] In addition, Beta Israel made efforts not to allow Christians into their homes. They especially avoided inviting Christian women, who were not separated during their bleeding periods, posing a risk of particularly virulent ritual contamination as menstrual blood renders the woman's entire immediate area impure.

In recent times, however, and particularly in the Gondar region, these rules of purity and impurity were less strictly observed. Even the practice of eating Christian food in the course of a shared meal was gaining acceptance, so long as the meal did not include meat. Still, many Jews, particularly among the older generation, were even stricter about avoiding physical contact with non-Jews.

In most regions where the avoidance of physical contact with non-Jews was maintained, a variety of strategies was developed to permit regular and even intensive interactions. Among these was the use of freshly cut branches employed as a mat on which Christians could stand when entering Jewish homes and as a buffer-barrier which could be touched simultaneously by Jews and non-Jews while working together in the fields.[5]

When Christians wished to give the Beta Israel money (as payment for handicrafts, for example), they might place the coin on animal droppings and the Beta Israel would take it from the dung. The droppings, they explain, canceled out the impurity. When a Christian woman came by to speak with her Jewish neighbor, she would call from outside the home. The Jewish woman would step out to the yard and converse with her Christian friend, who remained, all the while, on the other side of the fence. At times the Christian woman would be invited over for coffee, but she remained outside the fence and drank coffee which the Jewish hostess had prepared in a special cup made of clay. After the visit, the Christian woman would either take the cup with her or break it.[6] In other areas, Jewish families kept a second set of dishes for their Christian neighbors, dishes which were stored in the yard on a tree or a bush. Their neighbors were familiar with this practice and would take their own dishes whenever they came for a visit.

Many Jewish families maintained close ties with their Christian neighbors. In such cases, the Christian neighbors would keep a special set of dishes for the Jews as well. When members of the two groups participated in joint celebrations and rituals, measures were taken to permit the Jews and the Christians to be at the same site.

The practices of separation and avoidance of physical contact were rooted in the Beta Israel's view that the Christians were unclean because they did not maintain the rules of purity practiced by the Jews. Nonetheless, we find a wide array of practices whose purpose was to permit proximate relations with the Christian neighbors. The names by which the Christians referred to the Jews were understood by the latter to reflect the same ambivalence of attraction and repulsion. These names communicated to the Beta Israel, in a direct, face-to-face fashion, the many ways in which they were perceived as different by their non-Jewish neighbors. The name that I employ in this study, "Beta Israel," though the name of choice in the eyes of the group itself, was rarely used by Christians in daily interactions. This may indeed be one of the reasons the Ethiopian Jews preferred it: the appellation "Beta Israel" parallels "Beta Christian," the name for the Christian house of prayer in Ethiopia. Thus, it symbolically places the two groups on a similar footing by allotting equal weight to each, at least phonetically. At the same time, their use of the word "Israel" evoked the view that Jews were the direct descendants of an ancient people. This, in turn, linked them to the mythological bond between King Solomon and the Queen of Sheba, the progenitors of the Amhara, who have dominated Ethiopia in the present century. Indeed, the ruling dynasty in Ethiopia described itself as being led by the king of kings, lion of Judah, and elect of God.

The appellation "Agaw" stood as a binary opposition to the name "Beta Israel." It was used often by the Christians, especially in the Tigre and Wolqait regions. Agaw is both the Cushitic language perceived as predating the Ethio-Semitic languages and also a general name popularly used for the pagan groups which inhabited pre-Christian Ethiopia and for those still present.[7] Calling Ethiopian Jews Agaw delegitimized their claim to having originated in Israel,[8] devaluating them, within Ethiopian cosmology, to mere pagans. At the same time, paradoxically, the otherwise derogatory name recalled the Agaw-Zagwe dynasty, which seized power from the Solomonic dynasty,[9] ruling Ethiopia for more than 200 years.[10] Nonetheless, the speakers, most of whom hailed from Wolqait and Tigre, agreed that "Agaw" was incomparably better than names applied to Jews in other regions:[11] "In Tigre they don't curse us. They merely call us *buda* and *kayla*. We have been in Tigre and Wolqait for forty generations."[12] "My family is the son of a son of a son, so they don't curse us that much."

"Falasha," the appellation best known to outsiders, was ranked by the Jews as close to "Agaw" in terms of the hostility and contempt it expressed. Its literal meaning is hard to capture.[13] Many Jews refer to themselves as Falasha when talking with one another, especially when discussing their lives in Ethiopia. The term's central significance has to do with their unlanded status, though symbolic meanings are added to this practical connotation. The symbolic meanings are related to their being strangers and perhaps even invaders, occupying land that did not belong to them. Thus the term took on a connotation similar to that of the "wandering Jew"—Jews punished by God by dispersal to the ends of the earth.[14]

The most mysterious appellation for the Jews of Ethiopia is the pejorative term *kayla*.[15] Its literal meaning is unclear, but its popular usage lends itself to a number of interpretations. The Jews who came to Israel from the Lasta and Wogera regions apparently employed it when talking among themselves about life in Ethiopia. Similarly, in the Belesa region, the term *kayla* was seen as a synonym for Beta Israel and used frequently as a common name even in the course of our interviews. Most of the speakers viewed the term as derogatory, as Christians used it for minority groups to whom they attributed supernatural powers. The term came to be used against the Jews of Ethiopia because it had acquired some supernatural implications. Its very lack of substantial meaning and clarity indicated to the Jews that the accusations connected to the term similarly bore neither logic nor foundation. Even so, they struggled to understand why they were tarred with it and raised several conjectures. A handful of interviewees, mainly from the Tigre and Wolqait regions, attributed a historical-religious origin to the appellation and linked it to the religious isolation of the *kayla* from their Christian surroundings.[16] This understanding may be connected to the testimony of Abba Itzhak, a nineteenth-century monk, who suggested that the name referred to the mythological arrival of the Jews from the Land of Israel, and particularly to those who "did not cross the sea" when Menelik I, Solomon's son, and his people crossed the sea on the Sabbath.[17] Interviewees from the Tigre region also suggested that the term derived from the Hebrew *kehilla,* meaning "community" or "congregation." This folk etymology furnished proof in the eyes of the speakers that the first Jews in Tigre spoke Hebrew, a language forgotten by latter generations. According to these speakers, the forefathers of the group called themselves *kehilla* and the term was maintained even after they had forgotten the language.[18] Another common suggestion linked the term to a simple agricultural instrument: two sticks tied to a long wooden pole forming a V at one of its ends. This instrument is used to separate the wheat from the chaff and to uproot thorn bushes in the field. These thorns are sometimes called *kayla,* though the informants claimed that the word refers primarily to the wooden instrument itself. They also stated emphatically that they could see no connection between the Jews and either the instrument or the thorns.

Significantly, as an alternative to this collection of vague, menacing, and unintegratable meanings, the Jews suggested an interpretation entirely unrelated to magic. They derived the term from Beta Israel's original ties to Hebrew and Israel, their religious faith, and their agricultural pursuits. As such, it had no intrinsic derogatory implication. The gap between the insulting daily usage and the innocent original meaning of the appellation, as the Jews explain it, offers one more proof that the accusations made against them were vicious and false.

Chapter 3 will be devoted to an analysis of the most common appellations used by the Christians to describe the Ethiopian Jews—*buda, jib,* and *jiratam*—all of which refer to their supernatural powers.

Despite all rhetorical derogations, the Jews were actually indistinguishable from their Christian neighbors, both physically[19] and linguistically. Jews who lived in the Tigrinya-speaking regions spoke Tigrinya, in Amharic regions the Beta Israel spoke Amharic, and in areas in which both languages were spoken, such as the Wolqait (situated between the Amharic- and Tigrinya-speaking regions), they spoke both languages.[20] Thus, when Amharic-speaking Jews met Tigrinya-speaking Jews, they had no common tongue. The physical and linguistic similarity of Jews and Christians made it impossible to avoid contact. In trying to guard themselves against threats of contamination, Beta Israel invented some ingenious rhetorical strategies. One tactic dealt with the situation in which a Jew sought to recognize another Jew in public—without giving away the Jewish identity of either. Another tactic enabled the speaker to warn a fellow Jew that Christians were present.[21] In both cases, the Jews proudly recall, the words employed were secret codes, known only to group members.

These code words were drawn from two main sources: different dialects of the Agaw languages spoken by Beta Israel in earlier times, whose original semantic meaning was no longer known to most of the interviewees, and other terms taken from their unique in-group, vocational vocabulary, which the Christians did not understand.[22] In recent years, they also integrated Hebrew words they learned from Israeli-trained Ethiopians or other Israeli immigration officials.[23] The Beta Israel employed the term *shevet* (Hebrew for "tribe," as in the twelve tribes of Israel) to identify Jews, members of their group, and *goy* (Hebrew for "nation" but implying "non-Jew") to designate non-Jews, usually Christians. In cases in which there was some doubt as to the identity of another person, one could ask, *"Shevet?"* If the person answered in the affirmative, it was a sign that both speakers were Jews. *"Goy,"* on the other hand, was used to warn another Jew of the presence of a non-Jew, without making public what was being communicated. According to the informants, both words became current when Beta Israel teachers returned from training in Israel, replacing other words that had earlier served the same function.

A combination of attraction and repulsion characterized the complex relations between the Jews and their neighbors. Evident in everyday interactions, this dialectic was reflected in a wide-ranging and complex order of naming. As the names that the Jews acquired were labels applied by their Christian neighbors—most of them negative—the interviewees felt no need to give them a positive cast. Close examination shows that while the meaning of some names is clear, others are not given to a single interpretation. The Beta Israel's understanding and interpretation of the names formed a vehicle for them to directly address and evaluate boundary issues, on both the emotional and cognitive levels. Their way of relating to these appellations allowed them to formulate a perception of themselves in the eyes of the other and to mark their place in the Ethiopian context. Characteristic of this level of cultural articulation was a relatively narrow focus that ignored multidimensionality. The principal markers of this view moved along a spectrum of components: ethnic, historical, religious, ritualistic, and magical.

CHAPTER 2

Christian Land, Sabbath Milk, and the Magic of Fire

The interactions between Ethiopian Jews and their Christian neighbors were played out in a wide variety of everyday contexts and through media as diverse as land, milk, and fire. Through the familiar routines of daily life, larger issues pertaining to intergroup relations were enacted.

CHRISTIAN LAND

Most of the Beta Israel farmers were tenants on lands they leased from their Christian neighbors.[1] The relationship between Christian landowners and Jewish tenants survived in Jewish memory as similar, in principle, to that between Christian landowners and any other tenants. The ties were personal, familial, and based on various types of mutual agreements. Usually, the head of a Beta Israel household approached a landed Christian household and asked to lease a certain plot of land. The agreements between the two sides had to take into account a wide array of factors: the physical condition of the plot (its size, the quality of the soil, the level of investment required to realize its potential), as well as the supply and demand for land in the region.

The majority of the agreements were based on the tenants giving the owner a certain percentage of their crop each year as payment. The precise amount was determined by different considerations and ranged from one quarter to—in certain regions—a full half. Alternatively, a fixed amount of harvest was agreed upon at the outset. There were also progressive agreements, especially about plots that had not been tended for a long time. In addition, there were local agreements suitable to special conditions or relations between the two sides. Some of the agreements were in writing, while others were oral contracts, always made in the presence of witnesses from both sides.

In many cases, the relations between the Christian landowners and the Beta Israel farmers continued over several generations. An ongoing agreement—in the view of the Jews—was beneficial to both sides: the Jews gained financial security while the Christians were comforted by the knowledge that this particular Jewish family was not employing their supernatural powers against them.[2] The link also facilitated mutual help in the field, Jews and Christians working together on the same plot—particularly when planting and harvesting. During these seasons, Jews and Christians spent a great deal of time together, working, eating, and talking.

The Jews employed various practices to observe their laws of purity while working with Christians. It was accepted that they would eat *injera* (Ethiopian bread usually made of an indigenous grain called *tef*), fruit, vegetables, and coffee together, but never meat or dishes cooked in the pots of the other group. In regions where Jews adhered more strictly to these rules, great care was taken not to touch the Christians or any of the objects that were perceived as conductors of impurity. One man who came from such a region (Semien) explained: "When you plowed, everyone would help, it's very simple. They would help us as well. But if there was a dry piece of wood in the field and they touched it, we wouldn't touch it. Only if it was wet. We wouldn't even lift the dry stick. If it fell to the ground we would ask someone else to come over and pick it up."

The ties between the Jewish family and the landowner were preserved and strengthened through gift-giving rituals. Beta Israel would give iron products, or simple work tools, as well as knives for ritual slaughter forged on their anvils. Gift-giving rituals created a fixed framework of mutual commitment, a framework which was established as early as the time in which the tenant Jews approached the Christian landowner with the request to lease his land. In the words of one interviewee: "In order to get land you have to give the *goyim* many knives . . . the land, everything is in the hands of the *goyim*."

Gifts to the landowner were also given during ritual celebrations: on Christian holidays or at family celebrations. One of the interviewees from Tikil Dingay in the Armacheho region explained: "In our area, my grandfather received land from a Christian. Then he gave it to my father and my father also gave me the permit. The Christian's land remained in our

Figure 8.   Harvesting wheat in a Beta Israel village, 1970s. Photograph by
Arthur Leipzig, courtesy of Beth Hatefutsoth Photo Archive.

family . . . if you're a good person they don't stop. Each time I can give
him a bit as a present. The Christians know that we don't have land, so
they say, 'Take it and tend it for me.'"

As mentioned, the agreements differed according to the region and
the quality of the land. It was common knowledge among the people I
spoke to that the most difficult situation and the most onerous leasing
conditions were in Belesa and Wogera. In these regions, harsh accusations were made against the Jews, alleging that they used magic to harm
the Christians. A *qes* who lived in Belesa recalled:

> We didn't have land so the *goyim* would give us some plot to care for and af-
> ter some time when they saw we worked well and the land is good so they
> say to us, "Give me back my land." "Oh! I worked well," I'd say, "why do
> you take it? I'll give you money." But they don't want money. They want the
> land back. It's hard there. In all Ethiopia it's hard, but in Belesa it's harder.
> It's also hard in Wogera. . . . I did . . . all [the work] and in the end I gave so
> much. Also in Wogera the *goy* would even take our weeds to feed his cows
> and donkeys. That's the way it was, there was nothing we could do about it.

A person from Wogera recounted:

> The Christians take half of everything, even the chaff that's left over from the
> grain . . . even what grows between the wheat, if someone plants something

else. Even the husks that our cows ate the Christians wanted. And I couldn't do anything because I'm like their slave. Sometime I take one third and they take two thirds and it also happens that they take three fourths and I take one fourth. That's the way it is in Wogera because there's excellent land there, but if the plot wasn't that good I would have to plow it four or five times, and then give half to him.

Even though the land was mostly Christian, the agreement provided that the Jews could decide when to renew or terminate it.[3] One of the interviewees explained: "Once the agreement has been made it holds until the Jew wants to go. The Christian wouldn't decide that the Jew should go since it's the Jew who pays every year and there are witnesses. So if the Jew doesn't want to continue he could go to another Christian or to a different region altogether."

This gives power to the party that is dependent upon the landowner for his livelihood. While landownership allowed the Christians a limited selectivity, it was the tenant who had the greatest freedom because he could always approach another landowner. A delicate and paradoxical balance results: the source of the landowner's strength is at the same time the source of his weakness, while the apparent dependence of the tenant is presented as a source of strength. This situation illustrates what some have called the "powers of the weak."[4] Many speakers noted, as mentioned before, that there was a common perception in Ethiopia that an unlanded person should be treated as someone with nothing to lose, and thus freer to take chances. The high degree of mobility that characterized Beta Israel in Ethiopia[5] reflects the search for new plots of land and easier sources of income.

SABBATH MILK

Cooperation between Jews and Christians in various aspects of husbandry was also common in all regions. The animals—cows, sheep, and goats—were tended either by Beta Israel youth or by Christian youth. In return for the care the Christians provided, they received both milk and manure. In various accounts the phrase "Sabbath milk" was mentioned. The agreements stipulated that Christians would milk Jewish-owned cows on the Sabbath for their own use. One man from the Tigre region explained: "A Christian can take the Sabbath milk of a Jew's cow. If there's a Christian neighbor nearby they let him take the milk. . . . We aren't allowed to drink or sell Sabbath milk."

"Sabbath milk" was also described as the milk given to the Christians who looked over the calves on the Sabbath because, as Jewish-owned livestock, the calves were forbidden from taking milk from their mothers on the day of rest: "You may not extract any milk on the Sabbath, you must not touch it. The Christian will take it for himself. A guard watches the children of the cow so that they don't touch their mother and take her milk."

THE MAGIC OF FIRE

A man recalled:

> Except for us, there are no Jews in Matrawa. All around just *goyim*. Only our family moved there, because we had no land. I had a good friend, a Christian, and he invited me. They asked me to work and live with them and make things from steel and cloth, since I know how to do those things. We wanted a field. We got along with the *goyim*. They went with their religion and we went with ours. I would make things from steel and wood together, like knives and plows, because the Christians don't know how to make those things. Later they asked me to move to their place. When we arrived there, there was a house ready for us to go in and during our last year [in Ethiopia], when our house was a little old, they fixed it for us. I would also make them rings not from gold and all sorts of things to wear not from gold. Also things to dig in the ground for agriculture and knives to cut the wheat. My second job was to make clothes and cloth. We grew our own food. We bought sugar, coffee, and salt. Except for those things we didn't need to buy anything. I work and my Christian neighbors give me what I need. If I need help in the fields, planting or bringing down the crop or cleaning the weeds out, they would do it for me. We grew potatoes, and they planted tomatoes for me, because only I was there to make things [crafts], so they gave me much honor. Do you know how much they cried when we left [for Israel]?

This account describes the strong bond between one Jewish family and its Christian neighbors.[6] Their work as artisans, and their specialization in specific branches of artisanship, characterized the Beta Israel to such an extent that a number of researchers suggested they be viewed more as a professional caste than as members of a different religion.[7] The landed Christians avoided these crafts because they were considered demeaning.[8]

Beta Israel men specialized in weaving and smithery and the women in pottery. The latter two occupations employed fire. People who worked with fire were considered to be endowed with magical powers.[9] To the

Christians, the power to transform otherwise useless things into useful objects by means of fire was surely supernatural. If they could change the form and function of things, what might they also do to people—including themselves? Rural communities needed the agricultural tools, knives, and clay vessels produced by the Beta Israel, and the eerie skills attributed to their makers endowed the products with a magical aura.

These skills earned the Jews the appellation *tebib(an),* a name that refers to artisanship, especially those crafts tinged with supernatural powers. The meaning refers to a "possessor of secret knowledge."[10] This power made the artifacts produced by Jews valuable and attractive but made their craftsmen suspect. "They call us *tebiban Israel,*" said one interviewee. "What does that mean? It means that we know how to perform crafts. That's the meaning. So it's not really a curse, but it's tied to a curse because *tebib* are people who perform manual labor and they know that people who do that also 'eat.'"[11]

The relations between the Jewish smith and his clients had much in common with those of the tenant and the landowner. Ties could span generations. It was quite common for there to be an arrangement that linked agriculture and artisanry: a Christian family allowed a Jewish family to work its land, the Jewish smith would supply the tools, knives, and at times even weapons. These products were viewed as part payment for the lease or the agreed share of the produce that the tenants owed the landlords.

Even when the ties were not close, it was common for each Christian family to have a preferred Jewish smith. The ties were based on mutual loyalty. Smiths whom I interviewed reported that they would not work for people who were known to be clients of another smith. According to them, the Christians also preferred to turn to "their" smith, since they counted on him not to harm them with his supernatural powers.

We have cited friendlier aspects of interdependence between a Jewish smith and his Christian clients. In other cases, particularly in the Belesa and Wogera regions, relations were far less idyllic. The interviewees spoke of instances in which they were exploited and received no payment whatsoever: "The *goyim* would come to our house and since they don't know how to make a plow they would ask us to make one and say that they'll pay after they finish working. When they're supposed to pay they say, 'This is *our* land, you shouldn't even *be* here.'"

In these places the supply of iron tools to the Christians took the form of tribute levied by contemptuous "lords of the land."

Figure 9.   Jewish potter, Ethiopia. Photograph by G. Sabar-Freidman.

Figure 10.   Jewish blacksmith, Ethiopia. Photograph by G. Sabar-Freidman.

Figure 11.   Jewish potter. Photograph by G. Sabar-Freidman.

BETA ISRAEL LAND

In a few regions, such as the Tagadi in Tigre and Wolqait, some Jews *did* own land. Their plots had been given to them in previous generations by the emperor or local authorities in return for their contributions in construction, carpentry, or military service.[12] In these regions the Jews even employed members of other groups (including Christians) as tenants. When Christians tended the fields of Jews as tenants, they were bound by an agreement which prohibited working on the Sabbath:

My father had a plot of land which he received from the mayor of Wolqait. There were no papers of ownership but everyone knows it's his. They have a belief over there, if someone gives his word that's stronger than a contract. It was from generation to generation. So my father had a serious plot of land . . . my father took both Jewish and Christian workers. But he absolutely prohibited their working on the Sabbath.

Nonetheless, there were informants who spoke of Christian attempts to strip them of these plots—especially those whose ownership was not established in a written contract but passed down orally from generation to generation. In such cases, the Beta Israel had no legal protection. As one speaker put it: "The Christian could take our land and it didn't matter if it's my father's land."[13]

In order to protect their land, the Jewish owners had to resort to informal tactics such as bribes and personal threats. One of the most detailed accounts dealt with a specific incident in which the Christians demanded use of land owned by Beta Israel in Wolqait. The speakers emphasized that everyone (including the Christians) knew that the plots had been given to the Jews. When the matter came before a local judge, the local dispute over a specific plot of land was blown up into a general debate over the landowning rights of Jews versus Christians:

> The Jews had this land and suddenly, without discussing anything, the Christians started to demand it. And we know that it's ours and everyone else knows it too. So we told the Christians that it's our land. My brother was sort of a leader and he was a good speaker. So when he went to court . . . my brother had to prove that the land belonged to the Jews. There were old Christian witnesses he dragged in because they also know. They can swear on the New Testament. He took old witnesses and asked them in the trial whether these lands belonged to Jews. That was the point of the trial because the Christian asked in the trial how could it be that the Jews suddenly showed up and came to Ethiopia. So my brother had to go back to history, saying that the first to come to Ethiopia had been the Jews. But the Christians paid the government a lot of money in order to take the land from us. So what did we do? We saw that it's not going to remain ours. So my father started to tend the land himself, and they couldn't tell him to move. Why? Because if they tried to evict him he'd sue them for another matter. For what? He told them he remembered when they had taken some of our girls, raped them, and turned them into Christians. He said he would find out who their children are. He said: "I have a list from the days of this and that king and I want to expose who their children are." It happened that the mayor himself was one of these children. So the mayor asked them to hush up the whole business. . . . He didn't want anyone to know that his mother's mother was a Jewess. So he wanted to hush up the business. He left that land with my father and said that he, himself, would find a way to take care of the Christians.

The man who told me this was visibly frustrated with the Jews' status in Ethiopia. Even in the regions where the Jews were landowners, their ownership as shaped in their memories was neither stable nor assured. They lived under threat of expropriation by their Christian neighbors— threats which utilized fabulous claims regarding the historic illegitimacy of the group. Furthermore, the counter-tactic employed by Beta Israel was almost ironic. Their only recourse was rattling historical skeletons in the personal closets of local leaders.

The main locations on the (re)collective map of daily relations between the two groups coalesce around a number of seemingly disparate sites. The interviewees' descriptions of these points of meeting belie a fundamental ambivalence, rooted in the inseparable tangle of relations: land, agriculture and husbandry, husbandry and religious practice, religious practice and religious belief, belief and artisanship, artisanship and magic, and so forth. Society was hierarchical and professions were ethnically defined, but close daily interaction persisted nonetheless. The quotidian relations and their interlocking ties generated considerable difficulties for the Beta Israel, who found them complex and confusing. This confusion and lack of consistency in the relations between the two groups was a source of ongoing struggle. The coming chapters will continue to trace other, indirect expressions of these relations, demonstrating how these inconsistencies are decoded, shaped, and reshaped in the perspective of the interviewees.

CHAPTER 3

The Jew as *Buda*

Hyena in Human Form

"Night had just fallen on my village," narrated one of my Ethiopian friends.

> I was finishing up at my forge . . . a terrible knocking at my door—a crowd of angry neighbors burst in screaming, "Come with us now!" "What happened?" "You know." What could I do? I went. When I saw smoke pouring from my neighbor's house, I knew. They pushed me through the door. I saw my neighbor's little son lying in his bed. He looked feverish. He shook when he saw me. "You did this to him!" his family cried. "Make it go away. Apologize." The Christian said I was the *buda* who ate him. The child told them. They asked him again and again. They made smoke to help him see who did this to him. You understand? He had to say something, so he said it was me.

I learned that the interrogation could go on for hours. I also learned how central a place magic holds in the Ethiopian cosmology.[1] Alongside simple mortals there are supernatural entities, often combining human and animal characteristics in unpredictable ways. All are endowed with magical powers. Beta Israel's neighbors viewed them as belonging to the latter group.[2] The boundaries between the animal, the human and the divine, were vague and indistinct and could be crossed with fatal results.[3]

The magical cunning of Beta Israel was associated with the *buda*, the mythical hyena that figured centrally in Ethiopian supernatural cosmology.[4] This cannibalistic figure is associated with artisans, and smiths in particular. The hyena-man and other human / animal transformations connected with the supernatural are not exclusive to the Beta Israel. Similar associations attach to other groups throughout Ethiopia and across Africa.[5] But as I explore in this chapter, the concrete accusations which link the *buda* and the Beta Israel, according to the recollections of my interviewees, take on a unique dimension not found in other African contexts. The specific contents attributed to the Beta Israel *buda* integrate accusations associated not only with their profession but also with Beta Israel's religious tradition and the conceptual differences between Judaism and Christianity in Ethiopia.

According to one widely held view, the *buda* disguises itself as human during the day but reverts to its original form at night. The informants emphasized that in the Christians' eyes, the natural state of the *buda* is that of a hyena and not of a human. The appellations *jib,* meaning "hyena," and *jiratam,* meaning "tail," refer directly to this image. These were considered the most offensive appellations, since the hyena image, and in particular the choice of this animal's tail, the most ridiculous and "extraneous" part of the animal's body, serves to dehumanize and ridicule the Jews.

The view that the original form of Beta Israel is that of the hyena bespeaks a total dehumanization of the Jews. Being hyena-people, the Beta Israel were feared for their "eating," that is, their sucking the blood of living victims or of recently buried cadavers, which they disinter and use to satisfy their nutritional and ritual needs. The "eating" is done by casting an evil eye on the victim, who feels as though his blood has been sucked.[6]

Though the entire group was suspected of maintaining ties with supernatural powers and was called by names which refer to this, there were individuals and families to whom far greater power was attributed. People working with fire were considered more dangerous. Their power could be passed on "genetically" to their children.[7]

Those informants who were accused of harming someone through magical powers spoke of the accusation as a mark of shame on their family for many years: "If they accuse me of using supernatural forces, it takes away my honor and the honor of my children for generations."

Defending against the *buda* required first and foremost physical separation and distancing. It was necessary to avoid eye contact: a master of the evil eye could "eat" you. Similarly, Christians covered their faces with kerchiefs when they approached the *buda* and hid their children— the *buda*'s victims of choice—behind their backs. More active defenses included lighting a fire and producing smoke (*goma*)[8] as a means of stopping and even chasing away the *buda*. Smoke was sometimes used on a victim whose spirit had become one with the *buda*'s spirit[9] to reveal who had "eaten" him.

Smoke could be generated by burning tires or chicken droppings mixed with an assortment of woods. The Christians knew that on market days Beta Israel, and the artisans in particular, passed through their villages, so they lit *goma* in front of their houses.[10]

The diagnosis and care of evil-eye victims required ascertaining the perpetrator's identity. While administering smoke therapy, the victim was asked, "Who ate you?"[11] The victim would usually name one of the smiths or potters who lived near him. The "guilty party" would be summoned to face the victim and forced to apologize and retract the injury. On a number of occasions, an article of the *buda*'s clothing was taken and thrown into the fire. It was then given to the victim, who inhaled the smoke rising from the burnt cloth. This smoke was said to aid in his recovery.

These were common occurrences in their villages, and many informants had to face situations in which they were expected to beg for forgiveness from an ill Christian. The consequences of dismissing the accusations could be severe, as many speakers explained:

> If they have a sick child they say, Tell us who did it to you, and then they put him in the smoke and tell him to talk. He has no choice so he talks. He *lies*. He says that so and so did it. Then they come to you and say, "Apologize, apologize that you ate him." So you have to go, otherwise they kill you. You can't refuse to go because everyone believes it, including the government, so you have no choice but to go.

The accusations that the Jews possessed magical powers had a powerful influence on the relations between the two groups. The fear of Beta Israel's supernatural powers moved the Christians to maintain their distance. The specific content of the accusations against Beta Israel combined the occupations typical of the group and their unlanded status with their religious belief. Religious-historical tales were cited as evidence of Beta Israel's supernatural powers and of the manner in which they employed them against the Christians as proof linking the Jews with the scriptural events. As already mentioned, the Jewish smith is regarded as a descendant of the Jew who forged the nails for Jesus' crucifixion. Because it was set down in Holy Writ, the accusation was viewed as incontrovertible. As the progeny of the Jews who crucified Jesus, Beta Israel were accused of a continuing malevolent intent—an intent which passed from generation to generation. It was "in their blood," even without their being aware of it.

In the same fashion, the Christians interpreted the sacrifice of sheep—a rite central to the Beta Israel celebration of Passover—as the annual reenactment of the crucifixion. Anti-Jewish accusations already familiar from other cultural contexts, and in particular the killing of Jesus on Passover and the ritual murder of Christian children by Jews,[12] joined with magical conceptions which flourished in Ethiopia, creating a multileveled system of confirmation. The pan-Ethiopian myth regarding the *buda* is tied to creation itself. The *buda* was one of Eve's thirty children. According to this widespread story,[13] deeply rooted in Ethiopian folklore and narrated to me during the interviews, Eve hid her fifteen most beautiful children from God. Because of this they received no divine inheritance and God cursed them by turning them into animals, leaving their fifteen siblings in human form.

A psychoanalytic reading of this creation story reveals two themes:[14] Oedipal competition and sibling rivalry. It was God who originally divided the *buda* from the Amhara. Like Abel, the Amhara were blessed. Like Cain, the *buda* was rejected and cursed. The relations between the *buda* and the Amhara also reflected fear and instability between rival groups that are mutually interdependent, doomed to live in close proximity. The unlanded *buda* exemplified a people deprived at once of human identity and of land—all this due to the will of a stronger brother and an unforgiving Father who preferred one son over the other.

In this context I was startled to learn that in a typical hyena litter of two, the stronger cub often fatally attacks and eats the weaker, while the mother either does nothing or actually aids the attacker. A number of recently published biological articles discuss this phenomenon.[15] Such sibling cannibalistic behavior is unusual among mammals. Although never directly mentioned in the interviews, I suggest that this fact may have bearing on the complicated conceptual matrix involved in these magical accusations.

In projecting this image onto the Jewish group, the psychoanalytic reading takes on a more profound dimension. The Oedipal competition and sibling rivalry are superimposed on a more fundamental struggle for religious legitimacy. After all, both religions were fathered by the same God. Moreover, the rivalry was embittered further by the fact that Beta Israel had no land in Ethiopia. For the Beta Israel it was as if they had been disinherited by the curse God placed upon them in preferring the Christians over them.[16]

The *buda* and the Jews, both of which are described in Ethiopian myths as the crucifiers of Jesus, are viewed as a single entity. In another version of the crucifixion, it was the *buda* who drove Jesus out of his hiding place with two attached sticks, while the smiths provided the nails with which he was fastened to the cross.[17] For this, and for their original rejection of Jesus, the Jews merited punishment. Tried and convicted by God, they were punished by history.

Anti-Jewish accusations, familiar in other contexts, were woven into a prevalent magical cosmology, confirming beliefs regarding the harm Jews and Judaism inflicted on Christians and Christianity, and fully justifying the stringent defensive measures taken against them. In many of our conversations, speakers tied these magical accusations to the origins and rise of Christianity in Ethiopia. Thus—although in a completely opposite meaning—the Jews displayed a view which shares much, on the symbolic level, with the Christian conception of the links between their Jewish belief and supernatural powers. Here too the accusations were tied to God's desire to punish the Jews, albeit for a limited time, perhaps, I was told, as a "test with which God is testing the Jews" while at the same time granting Christians power.

CHAPTER 4

Gift Giving and the Multiple Meanings of Knives and Sheep

Strange as it may seem, the chaotic realm of accusation, dehumanization, and fear coexisted with another realm, the ritualistic, characterized by cooperation and conviviality.

A man from the Gondar region recalled:

> If I have Christian friends I can invite them. If there's eating I give them a sheep for as many as are coming and they slaughter it alone, on the side. Each side sits alone, also the Muslims eat alone. Then when there's happiness and dancing, everyone joins together. . . . Now if, for instance, the Christians have a wedding, then I can't go in when they're eating. . . . If he gives a whole sheep and we're not that many people then I take it home. After I took it home, maybe on Thursday or Friday I'll kill it. Then my whole family eats it.

Following the meal, everyone gathered in the central *das,* a special open hut built for ceremonies, and danced and sang for many hours. Hospitality customs were based on mutual acquaintance. Each group knew the other's rules and adhered to them scrupulously. With areas of cooperation and separation clearly defined, neighbors could indeed "enter" the social framework created by wedding rituals.

WEDDINGS

Neighbors from different groups were most commonly invited to attend wedding ceremonies. The event was divided into two distinct parts: the religious ritual and the celebration. Generally, according to the Beta Israel recollections, the religious part was not attended by the guests from the other group, and the festive meal was held separately, but in physical proximity. Special huts were erected for each group so they could dine separately. Each group only ate meat that it had slaughtered.[1] Consequently, when guests from a neighboring religious group were invited to a celebration, the hosts supplied the invited parties in advance with animals for slaughter as well as with the ingredients to prepare *injera* (bread) and *tella*, a beer usually made from barley—the elements that were the staples of every festive meal. When Christians were invited to a Jewish wedding, they received an animal which they then slaughtered and cooked *during the ceremony*, using pots and cooking utensils they brought with them. When, on the other hand, Jews were invited to a Christian wedding, their representative was given the animal ahead of time, usually a few days prior to the celebration. The Beta Israel then cooked the meat in advance and divided it among the invited Jewish families, each taking its share home.

There were regions in which the guests' participation was more segregated. Joint dances were prohibited, and one could only watch the dancing. A woman from the Seqelt region:

> If we have a wedding we invite the Christian neighbors. Before the wedding I gave them sheep, they have a *qes* and they perform the slaughtering on their own, far far away. And I [meaning the Jews] also slaughter far away. Then there's beer, and I gave some to them. I also gave them *injera* alone, that I had made. But if she invites me and she prepares the *injera*—I don't eat. If in a wedding I give them a sheep to slaughter and they eat it, we can't dance with them. Dancing is on the side [separately], and even if I go to their wedding and they dance I stand on the side and do like this [claps hands and sings], but don't dance with them.

When I asked her why it was so, she answered: "It's prohibited. It's blood in the house! It's prohibited to touch each other. If you dance you can touch, so it's prohibited."

While in certain regions or among certain families there was a more stringent avoidance of physical contact, this did not disrupt the mutual participation in celebrations which were so central to intergroup relations in Ethiopia. The two sides were aware of what the members of the other group were and were not permitted to do and tried to cooperate as much as possible with their rules. Thus, for instance, during fast periods for the Christians, and particularly when they had to give up meat for Lent, the Jews served other types of food.

The Christians, as construed in the memories of many of the people

I spoke with, took care that Beta Israel, in this particular ritualistic context, could maintain their rules governing slaughter and eating: "They were very respectful from a religious point of view. They know what is permitted and prohibited. They would not try to force us. They gave us everything we needed in advance."

Inviting members of the other religion was, then, common practice to promote mutual familiarity and respect. Indeed, both groups made efforts to facilitate their neighbors' inclusion in the ceremony. The wedding also specified areas of separation. The steps of this "dance" of inclusion and exclusion carried over into the rules governing gift giving.

While members of the inviting group customarily brought only money, guests from other groups brought both money and a gift. The money was given to the celebrating family to help cover the great cost of organizing the event, functioning like a flexible "bank," raising a large amount of money in a short time. The amount of money given by each participant was scrupulously recorded to ensure a reciprocal commitment. These agreements transcended religious boundaries. In addition to money, wedding guests from neighboring groups also brought other gifts[2] that were typically given by members of each group on such occasions.

"THE GIFT OF A JEW"

Nonmonetary gifts carried particular symbolic meanings charged with hidden messages.[3] Very often the Beta Israel gave knives to their Christian hosts a few days before the wedding, to enable their use at the ceremony. As one speaker explained: "If the Jew works with iron, he brings iron knives to the wedding. . . . He might bring three or four knives as a gift. That is the gift of a Jew."

The speakers drew a clear distinction between the different types of knives they made. There were curved knives *(kara)* used in daily agriculture; there were long, straight knives *(marejiya kara)* for animal slaughter; and there were smaller, more personal knives, rather like pocketknives *(billawa),* considered luxuries and used to cut meat, though not for slaughter. A Jew usually brought one of these to his Christian landowner when tenancy was established.

There were two kinds of *billawa,* or personal knives. One was double-edged; the other sharpened on one side only. When a *billawa* knife was given as a gift from the Jew to the Christian, it was invariably single-edged. The rationalization for this was: "If you bring a knife that is sharp on both sides, that is dangerous for him. A one-sided knife only he can use." The sharp side of the knife represented the receiver's domination, the dull side the Jew's subordination. The knife exchange struck me as odd: that the subordinate group should choose to pay tribute to the dominant group with a gift less powerful than that which they themselves used. A further meaning was apparently embedded in this exchange. While the ostensible message was tribute and honor, the latent message was an exhibition of unexpendability and strength, since it implied a reverse dependency. The dominant group relied on the Jews to provide their basic tools and perform the tribute ritual. The single-edged knife, then, had a double- edged meaning. Consider a widely told legend, much enjoyed by Ethiopian Jews:

A delegation of Christian notables came to Emperor Téwodros (II)— the "King of Kings," who ruled Ethiopia from 1855 to 1868—and asked him to annihilate all the Ethiopian Jews. The ruler arranged a debate at his palace, with both sides sending their representatives.[4] The emperor invited them to dine with him. Appetizing meats were laid before the guests, but there were no knives. Staring at the meat, unable to eat it, the Christians understood Téwodros' message and gave up their plan to destroy the Jews.

As a tool which can also be used as a weapon, a knife is a highly charged object.[5] The Beta Israel articulated this tension even when they referred to knives in a different frame of reference. If a knife appears in a dream it is understood as a sign, as a divine message, with possibly ambivalent implications. For God, it was said, "guards with a knife but also threatens with it." When the Jews bring money to Christian weddings they are establishing their unconditional support. But when they add the gift of a knife, they are simultaneously representing themselves, in a subtle but concrete ritualistic context, as a potential threat.

Ethiopian weddings bond people from different families, different villages, and in some cases even distant areas and languages. A wedding anticipates children and heirs. Inviting the landless and politically powerless Jews to a fertility rite uniting masters of the earth honors the perpetuation of Christian dominance and highlights the Jews' subordination. At weddings, the Beta Israel traditionally give the knives that are unexpendable to agriculture and animal husbandry, symbolizing fertility. The unstated fact that only the Jews make knives carries a rather less submissive message. With it the Jewish guest is quietly reminding his host that he is, in fact, indispensable, that this is symbiosis—not merely subordination.

According to the hermeneutics of the Beta Israel, by bringing a live sheep to a Jewish wedding, the Christian landowners present themselves as providers, as "nature." The Beta Israel depict themselves as "culture," the producers of the tools needed for agriculture or slaughter—to transform "substance" into "sustenance." In this way, they emphasize the tremendous dependence of the Christians on the products they make and, on the symbolic level, on the Beta Israel themselves.

The knives represent their makers well: their production is thought to be despicable and, according to the Ethiopian belief, linked to the supernatural. But at the same time a knife is necessary, and—precisely because of its supernatural provenance—possesses a special quality. It is simultaneously despised and necessary, threatening and protective. The choice of the type of knife, in conjunction with the ritualistic context in which it is given, emphasizes, from the many facets of their complex relationship, the cooperation and symbiosis between the two groups.

The gifts given by both groups at weddings constitute two poles on a doubly transformative continuum running between the live sheep and the knife, and between the Christians' earth and the Beta Israel's work on it. This dual continuum is linked by a double bond of nature / culture transformations. The transformative encounters between the earth and those who tend it, and between the knife and the sheep, constitute a bidirectional intersection of nourishment and fertility. The intersection is manifested in the exchange of gifts that bear a message of symbiosis and cooperation, anchored within the appropriate ritualistic framework, that of marriage. There is a degree of congruence between the structural level of gift giving as a framework of mutual commitment and the level of symbolic interpretation of the specific gifts. From the array of available contradictory meanings, those chosen are related to intergroup cooperation and commitment.

CHAPTER 5

Christian Help with Jewish Dead

Mitigating the Crisis of Impurity

Death in Ethiopia is dealt with in two ritual phases: the burial—*qaber*—and the *tazkar,* or remembrance day, a rite to raise the soul of the deceased. According to the interviewees, their Christian neighbors participated in both ceremonies, but while the *tazkar* services did not usually draw many Christian participants, they often attended the burial ceremonies and played a central role in the ritual.[1]

When a Jew died, his or her relatives and neighbors would announce the death and the time of the funeral to the Jews in surrounding villages. The message was delivered orally by young men, who departed as heralds and passed the word to as many villages as possible.[2] Due to pan-Ethiopian magical beliefs associating the liminal period between death and burial with danger,[3] the heralds traveled in pairs and did not eat or drink until after the funeral. Christian neighbors, also in pairs, joined in transmitting the news, and also fasted until after the burial. The Christians who went off to spread the news knew the villages in which the Beta Israel lived, and even the precise location of their homes.

In the memories of the interviewees, the role of the Christian neighbors in the burial ceremonies was even more central. In many cases it was Christians who carried the body on a wooden "stretcher" borne by four men. The cemetery was often shared by a number of inhabited villages or located near distant abandoned villages. The walk from the deceased's hut to the Jewish cemetery could thus take as long as several hours. The Jews were very strict in their observance of the laws protecting them from the "impurity of the dead." According to these laws, anyone who came in contact with the corpse had to spend seven days in solitary confinement in a separate hut and be purified with the ash of a red heifer[4] on the eve of the seventh day. Only then could he return home.

The Christians, who were, in the consciousness of Beta Israel, familiar with these strict laws agreed—indeed, offered—to help with the bearing of the deceased. The central reason for this aid, according to the Jewish interviewees, was the Christians' desire to avoid losing such a significant workforce for seven days. In this manner, many people were "spared," as only the two Jews who cleaned and prepared the body for burial became impure. Upon arrival at the cemetery, the Christian neighbors entered and even helped to dig the grave and lay the body in it. After the body had been interred, the ceremony was run solely by Beta Israel. During the seven days of mourning that followed, Christian neighbors would visit the grieving family and express their condolences.

The Jews would likewise participate in the burial of their Christian neighbors, but theirs was a more passive participation, joining with the crowd of mourners who walked behind the body up to the entrance to the cemetery. They would wait outside the cemetery, located adjacent to the church in many villages, until the end of the ceremony, when they joined the mourners leaving the area.

Ethiopian Jews who spoke of this mutual participation emphasized the lack of symmetry between the groups and their great dependence upon the Christians who bore the body. One man from the Felaswusgi region explained:

> They would help us a great deal with the carrying of the dead. My sister had a son who died, so the Christians took him halfway to Felaswusgi. It's heavy for them too, but they don't care. They don't take ritual baths, nothing. If one of ours dies, two people would take him and put him in the earth. Only these two people, and they [the helping Christians] don't sit in the [separate] hut for seven days [as we do]. The Christians can help us with carrying our dead. They would also cry and cry.

A *qes* from the Tigre region interpreted the asymmetry in the participation in burial ceremonies:

> The Christians can help us with our bodies but we can't help them with theirs. They can hoist on their shoulders and they can enter the cemetery. We can't. If a Christian wants to perform a good deed he can help lower the body into the ground. He doesn't care if he touches it or not. He touches corpses all the time. The Christian is like a cow. Does a cow care if it touches a dead body and makes its body impure? He can't come into our houses either, right after

he touched a dead body—only after a few days. . . . The Christian can hold
the cadaver on his shoulders if there aren't enough people to hold it and dig.
But he can't put it into the grave. He's allowed to come into our cemetery,
but he won't come stand right by the grave, [but] a little to the side. We also
go to the funerals of Christians, but we stand outside. We don't enter the grave-
yards. We stand outside the fence, then go wash.

This testimony contains a certain apparent tension. On the one hand,
the Christian is performing a good deed, yet in the eyes of the Jew, his
very act lowers him to the level of an animal. The dependency of the
Jewish community on the Christians for burial assistance thus engenders
a dehumanization of the latter. It is within this Jewish hierarchical framework that the people I spoke to chose to understand the resentment of
the Christians who helped with the funeral at this "injustice" (the informant's term). As "proof," informants cited Christians' unwillingness
on a number of occasions to help at all during burials. These reactions
began only during the lifetime of the interviewees, who indicated they
witnessed the change:

> The Christians come to our funerals and we go to theirs. We had a problem.
> The Christian can touch our deceased, but we couldn't touch theirs. It got
> very difficult for us on account of this. Once, there were good Christians. If
> someone Jewish died they would help by binding him and carrying him and
> digging in the ground for him. . . . But during the time of Haile Selassie the
> Christians said, "They hate us so we won't help them anymore."

My Ethiopian partners in dialogue believe that it became customary
for Christians to lend such extensive help in burying Jews during periods in which "many died," as in the terrible famine.[5] In using the term
"hate," the speaker was referring to the perceived feeling of Christians
that the Jews view them as inferior since they have no prohibition concerning physical contact with the dead.

In order to adjust to perceived increasing Christian reluctance to han-
dling Jewish corpses, the Jewish community devised methods to circumvent human contact with the bodies:

> The Christians once helped but [now] they are jealous. They say, "These
> people, even if it's their own father or their brother they won't touch him. So
> why should we? We won't touch either." They had to go very far to bury in
> so many different places (when many died). Back then they helped us but then
> they stopped. When the famine ended the sages of Israel made a new decree
> because we needed the Christians less. So what did we do? All our qesim[6]
> went to Abba Itzhak [the great qes of Tigre] to decide what to do. If you take
> a moist branch which is brought from a living tree, then other [Jewish] people
> can help. The impure walk one in front and one in back and the others use

green branches and help to carry as well. If it's wet it still has a soul [and thus can act as a barrier]. If it's dry then it's dead itself—impure.

Despite the introduction of the above solutions, the two religions continued to cooperate around matters of death. The Christian role as burial assistant clearly extended beyond simple technical aid, reflecting a much deeper significance to this moment in the relations between the two religious groups.

JEWISH PARTICIPATION IN CHRISTIAN FUNERALS

But even Beta Israel's relatively more passive participation in Christian funerals was considered a source of impurity. An immigrant from Tigre recounted: "Even though we didn't enter the cemeteries, we would bathe before and after the funeral ceremony. We would fast until the body was interred, not eating or drinking. Both the Christians and the Jews don't eat until the person is buried. It's so that He [God, via the dead man] will perform a *mitzvah* for us."

Despite the variety of customs and practices which revolve around the theme of purity and impurity, deeply ingrained in my informants' view of life in Ethiopia was the belief that their common God was grateful for human help in sending the dead to Him. For this reason, the mutual willingness to fast and to participate in the funerals of neighbors was thought to be rewarded in heaven.

The Beta Israel's strict enforcement of the rules regarding separation from the impurity of the body created a number of other difficulties. The impurity of participation took seven days, resulting in the loss of a week's work. At times, the vast distance which separated the cemeteries from the deceased's village made it necessary for the bearers to be supplied by local Christian villages.

When I heard of this arrangement, I couldn't help but wonder about the dynamics of the process. Why did Beta Israel depend on the Christians for this specific ceremony, when fresh branches could have been employed at an earlier time as well? How is it that the cause for reduced contact between the groups—the willingness of Christians to touch the dead—was what brought the groups together? What can we learn from the Christians' feelings as described by the Jews? Did they feel that the situation was not equitable and that they were being "taken advantage of" by Beta Israel, who utilized the Christian impurity to keep themselves pure? Perhaps this feeling reflects the Jewish conception that they themselves are purer than the Christians, whom they view as religiously inferior. Some sense of this may have registered in complaints of the Christians.

The practical argument for using the Christians' help had to do with the loss of work suffered by those who bore the body. But this too is curious. The Beta Israel send every woman to the "house of blood" for the same period of time every month. The loss of work is significantly greater, and still there has been no attempt made to find alternative solutions.

The joint attendance at burial rites may attest to the existence of a constantly evolving religious hierarchy within which the groups compete in their worship of a common God. Competition within this hierarchy is ongoing and integral to everyday relations between the groups. The joint participation in funerals—and the dichotomous situations of purity and impurity, life and death, which are part of them—constitute a symbolic dialogue of sorts regarding the religiosity of the two groups. As formulated in Beta Israel memory, Christians ascribed a religious value to the assistance they rendered at Jewish funerals, while the Jews viewed it as a religious violation. The fact that this dialogue took place specifically against the backdrop of burial customs is central to deciphering its meaning: it is here that a person passes from this world to the next, from a world in which religious differences are important to one in which the dead of all groups stand before the same Divine Judge.

CHAPTER 6

Religious Holidays

Inclusion and Exclusion

Religious holidays are yet another arena for the interplay of approaching and distancing. Beta Israel were thoroughly involved with the holidays of their Christian neighbors. They knew the names of Christian holidays, helping determine the precise day of the celebrations and at times even participating in them. The holiday cycle of the neighboring religions, and the Christians in particular, was integrated into Beta Israel's division of the year into holy and profane periods. The Beta Israel employ the holy days of other religious groups as markers around which their conception of time is arranged.[1] Moreover, the neighboring religious groups consult each other's calendars in order to better track the dates of their own holidays.

These are the words of a person who lived in Ambober in the Gondar region. The speaker's grandfather, a famous *qes*, was renowned for working out the dates of the holidays:

> My grandfather knew how to calculate the holidays. But he was also able to tell you today when there would be a full moon in three or four years. He was an expert. My grandfather began teaching me but I forgot. Look, the Christians count days. Each of their months has thirty days. Every month. They go by the days. They don't calculate according to the moon.[2] The Christians used to ask my grandfather lots of questions about the first day of our month. But there were also Christians who did know how to use the moon. They would ask us so that they would have their own holiday on the right day. Ours is a good reckoning, and they know it. I don't know why their reckoning is like it is, but when they set their holidays back then [at the dawn of Christianity] it was based on the Jewish holidays. At least I think it was. . . .

Figure 12.   Mother and daughter with the Passover *Haggadah* from Israel.
Photograph by G. Sabar-Friedman.

> So they kept their calendar and *always chased after the Jews' calendar. First
> they ask us and then they celebrate their holidays.*

Cooperation and mutual aid in setting the dates of holidays was not
exclusive to Jews and Christians. Beta Israel and their Muslim neighbors
use a lunar calendar. The Christians in Ethiopia count the months based
on a thirty-day cycle. Both the Christians and the Jews recognized the
proximity between the groups' respective holidays and had a general sense
of how each holiday was intertwined in the holidays of the other group.

FAMILIARITY WITH RELIGIOUS
PRACTICE AND MEANING

According to the informants, members of the various religions discussed
their neighbors' holidays and the symbolic significance of their customs.
One man from the Wolqait region said:

> Next to our Passover the Christians have a fasting holiday. It's called Arba-
> tom (Four Fasts). It's very long. For almost two months they don't eat milk
> or meat. They eat only *injera,* lentils and vegetables—that's permitted. But
> milk and meat are prohibited. It's a difficult fast. In the month of Nahase,
> which is winter in Ethiopia, the Christians also have a holiday during which
> they don't eat meat, but that holiday is only a week long. Muslims also have

Figure 13. Women with Passover bread, Walaqa, Ethiopia, 1984. Photograph by Doron Bacher, courtesy of Beth Hatefutsoth Photo Archive.

a month of fasting. All day they don't eat. Only at night they eat everything, including meat, and they drink until daybreak. They're very strong. At seven in the evening they eat and again at four in the morning, and then from five o'clock on they don't eat. That's the way they are. I saw it in Ethiopia and it's the same here [in Israel]. My Muslim neighbors would tell me everything, when they eat, when they can't eat.

This account demonstrates a sympathetic interest in the religious holidays of his former neighbors. Others expressed a certain discomfort or derision regarding specific aspects of their neighbors' customs. An interviewee from the Gondar region:

> They have a holiday known as Temqat—baptism. Christ was a Jew and he did Temqat in the water that made him a Christian. In this holiday they have something like our *Orit* and they have their *Tabot* [tablets of the law][3] that they put on their head or shoulders and they hold it and they shout and sing songs in Amharic. But no children. Only adult men and women and the *melekuse* (monks).[4] Like in a wedding. They dance a lot and sing a lot and pray. Then, in the morning, all the young men and women put black color on their eyes and color on their hands and legs, something they call *masusge*. They also put on earrings and necklaces, just like a bride. And they walk while we just watch. The Jews herding the sheep in the fields used to see it too. If they pass by our house we peek and sneak a glance. They throw holy water on everyone, even Jews! Look, Christ was a Jew and then became Christian. This water is a sign of conversion that someone was once a Jew or something and then became Christian.

This derisive description bespeaks the informant's ambivalence toward the Christian holidays and Christianity itself. Beyond the contrasting feelings of disparagement and approval evidenced in her account, the interview contains a wealth of significant hints about Beta Israel's attitude toward the Christians. When the speaker discusses Temqat, she refers—though not explicitly—to the centrality of the holiday which celebrates the most fundamental Christian transformation, that of a Jew becoming Christ. Immediately following that, she describes the central ritual of the holiday: The Christians dance together with the *Tabot* on their heads and shoulders "the way the Jews do with their *Orit*." Other informants speak of the "statue" or the "statue of Mary."[5] Another Jewish informant disparaged the use of "statues":

> At Temqat they take a statue out of their church and parade it through the entire village. They *cover it like our Torah*. You know how we hug our Torah? They do the same thing, hugging the statue with their hands while everyone dances in circles around the statue. Lots of people come out of the church and they circle through the entire village, just like we do in the Sigd. I think they also prepare some food by the church but not everyone eats, only their *qesim*. They also dress up and walk with umbrellas. But this statue is just wood, though they do cover it up nicely.

Any apparent similarity between religious practices was suspiciously scrutinized. For example, while the Jews pray holding a Torah codex[6] wrapped in cloth, the Christians hold a wooden icon similarly wrapped in cloth. The Torah of the Jews was perceived by the Beta Israel as divine; the Christian icon as a man-made God. Such close examinations were repeated over and over in Beta Israel accounts to exemplify the way in which superficial similarities disguise sacrilegious differences.

PARTICIPATION IN EACH OTHER'S HOLIDAYS

Clear rules governed participation in one another's holidays. Members of Christian and Muslim groups were not always free to attend Jewish holidays. Exclusions varied by region and holiday.

The holiday to which Christians were most typically invited was the Sigd. This holiday is unique to the Jews of Ethiopia: it is celebrated neither by Jews in other parts of the world nor by neighboring groups in Ethiopia.[7] It comes once a year, on the morning of the twenty-ninth day of the eighth month (according to Beta Israel's reckoning). At that time, the Jews gather in the main villages and towns, ascend a nearby mountain, where they fast, pray for mercy, forgiveness, and redemption, and read from the Holy Books. After the regional head *qes,* accompanied by fellow priests, delivers a sermon which includes both preaching and blessing, a festive meal is held. The polythematic nature of the Sigd has not yet been fully investigated, and the ecumenical implications encoded in it have not been explored.[8] For our purposes it is noteworthy that a large number of Christians participated, and prayers were said in public areas, in the presence of a large crowd, that included Christians and converted Jews. Although most of the people I spoke to recalled that the non-Jewish guests usually joined the ceremony after the prayers—that is, during the celebration and festive feast—there were a few intriguing reports of Christians participating in the prayers. According to the informants, their neighbors were familiar with the various stages of this holiday and knew the right times to join in.

The following detailed account from Ambober, a village in Gondar where a large Sigd ceremony was held, describes Christian participation in the Sigd:

> They don't pray, just look. We give them something to eat, over there, on the side. If, for example, we slaughter bulls we give each group according to their number. They stand on the side and listen to us during the prayers too. They listen from the beginning to the *qesim* pray. Some know Ge'ez and understand. Everyone listens: Jews, Christians, and Muslims. They listen and are very, very happy. They listen to everything from the Torah, from the *Orit.* . . . We translate it and they all stand and listen. The Christian *qesim* can also attend, I invite them to come. Look, as far as the other holidays are concerned, they knew when Passover was held. They would ask us on what day we're beginning Passover but they didn't come over to us on Passover, nor on other

Figure 14.   Men in the Sigd, Ambober, Ethiopia, 1984.
Photograph by G. Sabar-Freidman.

holidays. Maybe they would come but they'd stay outside, they couldn't come in. The Jews don't go to the Christians during the holidays—each person stays in his own home. Sigd *is completely different.* A lot of people from all different places would come to us. We also invited a lot of people so that they would come and see our holiday.

The Christian Meskel in Tigre, described from a Jewish point of view:

The Christians celebrate Meskel, which falls a little before we celebrate Sukkot (Feast of Tabernacles). This holiday is like Sigd[9] is for us. First comes our Yom

Figure 15.   The Sigd, Ambober, Ethiopia, 1984. Photograph by G. Sabar-
Freidman.

Kippur (Day of Atonement)[10] and then their Meskel. They sing, take the
wooden image of Mary to the river and dance there, and then they put her
back in the church. We go to watch. We don't eat. They were glad if we came
to them. Each would give you his spot, it's a sign of respect and honor.

These concrete examples, taken from everyday life, illustrate the attempt to coordinate the holiday schedules of each group as the Jews understood it. The holidays offered an opportunity for the expression of
affinity between Jews and Christians, while underscoring the concrete
and symbolic differences between them, by giving occasion for the comparison of customs and origins. The remembered practice of one group's
petitioning the other to pray on its behalf lent an additional dimension
to the importance of holidays in the relations between the groups.

PETITIONS FOR PRAYER

The Jewish Sigd celebrations were particularly significant for the non-
Jews. It was during this time that Christians asked the Jewish clergy to
pray for them. These requests were not reciprocated with similar requests
by Jews of the Christian clergy. The petitions were usually personal and
addressed to Beta Israel's religious clergy prior to the Sigd. Petitions might

include prayers to overcome infertility, to cure an illness, or even to harm one's enemy. Requests were also made on behalf of the entire community's agricultural needs: that rain either fall or cease, that hail not fall, and that there be no locusts. Such petitions were made during other periods as well, but the holidays in general and the Sigd in particular were viewed as most opportune. People I spoke with said that during droughts they themselves would turn to Muslim clergy who were considered "experts" in rainfall. But, they made a point of telling me, Jews never made personal requests to the Muslim clergy.

When Christians approached the Jewish *qesim* and asked that they pray for them, they proffered a preliminary gift. If their prayer was answered, the *qes* would receive an additional gift. While the preliminary gifts were usually of a personal nature—an animal, grain, or even money—an answered prayer would customarily bring a parasol, which acknowledged his religious authority. Donations included money for construction and maintenance in the *masgid*, various ceremonial objects such as fabric coverings for the Torah books; *gerdo* or *megarejja* fabric, which served as a curtain for the Ark, or for purchasing Bibles or religious literature.[11]

A man from Ambober reminisced:

> Once, for example, thieves were stealing a bull or a cow or money from a Christian. The victim would come to our Sigd. He would tell my grandfather that his possessions had been stolen and would ask him to pray for the death of the thief. He would say: "Pray for me, because God will hear your prayers." That's how the Christians would come to the Sigd. They used to bring us money and tell us that if the thief died next year they would bring more money. Muslims and Christians alike would come. It helps. I include it in the prayer in the Sigd and the Christian gives a garment for the Torah called *gerdo*. The Christian buys it if his thief dies, since that's a sign that the prayer reached God. He could also give us money or a garment for the ark which serves to conceal the Torah books. They also asked us to pray if it wasn't raining. In the morning we went to pray at this mountain we had and right away the clouds came. Quickly we ran home and said, "Look, God listens to the Jews." The Christians said, "Please, you pray, it only rains if the Jews pray."

In recounting how Christians asked for their prayers, the Jews could not conceal a certain bitterness. Only Christians could own land, but it took a Jewish prayer to bring the rain that would make this land fruitful. Politically weak and economically deprived, the Beta Israel were granted an aura of power[12]—particularly when that power could serve Christian advantage. This acknowledgment starkly challenged the notion that their religion had replaced Judaism as the one true path to God. The historical priority of Judaism was acknowledged, but its legitimacy

Figure 16. *Qes* with the *Orit* during the Sigd, Ethiopia, 1984.
Photograph by Moshe Bar Yuda, courtesy of Beth Hatefutsoth
Photo Archive.

was contested. The Christians' request of the Jewish priests that they
pray for them blurred dogmatic lines of separation and demonstrated
the complex intergroup negotiations regarding the legitimacy of each
religion.

Ambober and the mountain next to the village made up the site of the
largest Sigd festivities in the region, particularly in the years prior to
the mass immigration to Israel. It was viewed as a holy site from which
the path of the prayers to God was shorter.

A *qes* from Belesa compared his region to Ambober:

A Christian who doesn't have a wife or children would give maybe a *shekel*[13] to the Torah. That's what Christians do. They say, If I get a child within a year you get a golden parasol. *They give us a shekel and we put a clod of earth for them.* You give them a bit of soil. She puts it on her face and the following year she will have a child. Then she brings me a golden parasol. The Christian woman gives me the parasol. But that's in Ambober. In Belesa [the Christians] don't believe. They tell us the Jews are no good.

The prayer for children, in which the Jews took a piece of the earth they did not own and prayed over it in order to help the Christians to become fruitful and multiply, was like the prayer for rain, yet another blessing for fertility made by the Jews for their Christian neighbors.

The gifts given prior to the prayers are personal and comply with the rules that govern the gifts given by Jews to Christians at wedding ceremonies. And yet, once the request has been fulfilled, the Christians give the Jews religious ritual objects, which are signs of gratitude to the God who granted their wishes. These latter gifts express the recognition of the Jewish clergy's ties with the Divinity while encouraging Jewish worship.

Beta Israel integrated animal sacrifice in their rites; the Christians did not. Made aware by European missionaries[14] that mainstream Judaism had long ago abandoned the practice, the Christians, as the Jews recall, were highly critical of the survival of this discredited rite among their neighbors. At the same time, the Jews have a particularly vivid image of many Christians asking them to perform such a sacrifice on their behalf, which they understood as an acknowledgment of the special relationship between the Jews and God. The following dramatic account is from the Tigre region:

In 1950 there was a terrible bout of locusts in Ethiopia. At the time, *qes* Abba Itzhak of Maharia was living by us in Godolo (a village in the Adiaro province of Tigre). The Christians and the Muslims asked him to pray. They had a great Christian *qes* who was eighty years old and whose name was Gabrihat. He said that if the locusts persisted there would be a great famine, like when he was a child. He said to them: *"Go to the Jews and convince them. Even give them money, to buy a sheep, slaughter it for sacrifice and pray."* Then Jews said that we don't want their money since the locusts are bad for us too. We bought a goat ourselves and then everyone fasted for a day. We slaughtered the goat and didn't eat it. We put it on the fire, it was burnt, and everyone fasted. The locusts came in clouds and suddenly, all at once, the clouds turned away and went elsewhere.

The same event was recounted through the memory of a Jewish priest from the same region:

> You know, a while back there suddenly came a terrible plague of locusts. It was approximately thirty years ago. At that time the Christians asked *qes* Abba Itzhak (the great Jewish priest of Tigre) that we pray. Abba Itzhak and all the *qesim* and all the elders of the tribe prayed. We slaughtered a goat and burnt it as well, and fasted until evening. After that the locusts didn't touch any place inhabited by Jews. I don't know, but the locusts performed a miracle and didn't eat our crops any more.

The sacrifice of a goat to God illustrates the commercial nexus which exists between man and deity. The sacrifice of animals—just like the gifts given toward the maintenance, care, and beautification of the Torah and houses of prayer—are the presents mortals offer to God. The Beta Israel are perceived as fitting liaisons for this exchange—favored sons, as it were. This conception is expressed in the rhetoric of gift giving during religious holidays. It is utterly contrary to the ordinary disputes and disparagements which disfigured daily interaction between the groups.

The Beta Israel were equally critical, characterizing major Christian rites as irreligious and false compared to their own. This explained why God didn't respond to the Christians and why the Christians ultimately had no choice but to turn to them. These invidious comparisons were also aimed at establishing a clear hierarchy between the religions.

At the same time, the informants were impressed with the aesthetic aspects of Christian rituals, describing them with a mixture of admiration and disdain as if bereft of true meaning. Beta Israel's accounts of their neighbors' holidays were suffused with ambivalence. Despite this, prominent in the Jews' memory is the daily cooperation between the two groups. There was mutual knowledge of the other's holidays, cooperation in setting the dates, and physical attendance at the celebrations themselves. At the same time, and on a different level, they were described as bereft of true content and even their impressive external appearance sharpened their impression as showy and false.

The Jews took the view that the Christian holidays were improbable, even deceitful, notwithstanding the plethora of challenges and adversity their neighbors had to overcome to observe them. The supplications of the Christians to their idols went unanswered so they would plead with the Jews to mention them in their prayers, believing that these would be heeded.

CHAPTER 7

The Twice-Disguised Hyena

Under the influence of their Christian neighbors, many Jews converted to Christianity. When I was doing my initial research, this fact was virtually unreported. Later, when the extent of the phenomenon became public knowledge, a shrill debate ensued in the Jewish world, and particularly in Israel, as to whether the converts should be considered Jews and, in practical political terms, whether they should be brought to Israel. The information presented in this chapter was shared with me as part of a study of the speakers' lives, without consideration for the political ramifications of their statements.

Conversion was widespread. All the people with whom I spoke knew either individual Jews or entire Jewish families who had converted. The conversion of Beta Israel must be viewed as a multidimensional and multilevel phenomenon characterized by a number of different processes and a variety of motives, including the appeal of the Christian faith in Ethiopia, the influence of the Protestant mission,[1] the policy of specific leaders in Ethiopia, and the difficult material conditions and humiliation inherent in the life of Ethiopian Jews.

PERMANENT LIMINALITY

When people speak of their friends' conversions in Ethiopia, a number of central themes recur. The converts are described as inhabiting a state of permanent liminality,[2] somewhere between Judaism and Christianity.

Their conversion is never completed, they are "stuck" in the passage from one group to the other. The relations between Beta Israel, the converts, and Christian society, as positioned in the memory of the interviewees, are characterized by a high level of ambivalence, and the group's boundaries manifest tension between ethnic and religious criteria.

The passage from one religion to another involves, by definition, the departure from one status and the acceptance of a new one. Yet from the abundant data volunteered by the speakers, memory sketches a depiction of the converts remaining in a constant in-between state, even though they were baptized. The motivating factor strongly emphasized by the interviewees was not the decision to *substitute one religious belief for another,* but the desire to *belong to another group.*[3] The gap between expectations and reality following the conversion—a gap discussed time and again in several variations—maintains this inherent liminality. It was the pressure exerted by the Christians and the hope that such an action would improve their social and economic status that influenced the converts.

Discussion of these matters reveals the view that the conversion of individuals or whole families failed to "really change" them. The converts, it is said, remained Jews "within their hearts." The dominant Christian society continued to view them as a separate minority, even though they were no longer part of Beta Israel. They remained in a permanent intermediate category.

Three representative stories, the first by a man from Tigre, who studied for a while in Asmara:

> The Christians wanted to convince us. When I was in Asmara they would say to me: "If you convert we'll give you everything. If you enter Christianity I'll be your *avligi* [godfather], I'll get you things, I'll give you my daughter, I'll do this and that." Nobody in Tigre accepted. Nobody went. But in other places I know that many went. But those who did convert suffered a great deal, since they were lost in the eyes of the Jews, but the Christians didn't really accept them either. Whoever knew them when they were Jews had a difficult time accepting them as Christians. Inside, there was a sort of hate. Our parents separated us from the Christians. The Christians wouldn't even give him [the Jewish convert] their daughters. Then it became hard for us to touch their daughters. The [converted] Jew might want the Christian's daughter, but the Christian didn't agree. It is as if they put the converts in separate houses.[4]

An immigrant from the Maychew region recounted:

> Look, over there there's a reason for you to go [to the Christians]. It was very difficult because we didn't have land there. No land. You'll always be poor.

So if they don't have a way to make a living they might take the daughter of some rich man who has lands. But what happens? The Christian says come, I'll give you my daughter and I'll give you land. So then, after he converts to Christianity, he doesn't give him what he promised. Even when the converts' children play with the other children, the children know that the father is a Jew. One could pass through generations and never forget that he was a Jew.

An interviewee from the Wogera region narrated:

The Christians wanted us to do a *temqat* [baptism], that we should marry Christians and then we'd have land too. In Wogera they use land three times a year because the soil is very rich. It's the best land there is. That's why it worked that way . . . whoever went to them said maybe I'll be baptized and then go to the Christians. But my children won't be allowed to marry Christians. If you're *felasmuqra* [one of the names for Jews who converted to Christianity][5] then you have to find another *felasmuqra* to marry. The Christians don't marry them. In the beginning they tell you that they will let you marry them. Then they finish with the baptism and they don't let you. They always remember. If someone says "you ate someone," it's remembered for all the coming generations.

These accounts reveal that the attempt to plant hopes of a better life in the hearts of the converts never panned out. According to my partners in dialogue, the converts thus found themselves isolated in separate living quarters, with no choice but to marry within their own convert community. And of course they did not receive any land. Though it seems that in reality there were many variations, and in fact some admit that converts received lands, this nonetheless is the major implication of the interviews. Quite clear also is the Beta Israel feeling that the missionary fervor of the Christians was at least partially motivated by a desire to bring about their disappearance as faithful Jews. Many informants noted proudly that the Christians focused their missionary activity on Beta Israel and displayed little interest in members of other religions—Muslims, for example. The discussion of this situation is couched in terms of a rivalry between the two religions.[6] As the Jews put it, the Christians wanted it as proof that Judaism is disappearing. At the same time Christianity received additional legitimization and proof that it was the "true" religion after all. In addition, conversion manifested a repression, of sorts, of the Jews' potential political clout. In the eyes of the Beta Israel, the fear of their political power was anchored in historic traditions, according to which Ethiopia was ruled by the Jews in ancient times.

Despite the conversion, claim the speakers, the Christians continued to isolate converts and saw them as possessors of supernatural powers and, as such, potentially threatening.

RICHLY TEXTURED AMBIVALENCE

Emerging from the descriptions of the interviewees is the notion that the ongoing relations between the converts, Beta Israel, and Christian society were marked by profound ambivalence. Many speakers emphasized the historical changes in the nature of conversion. While in the past it was common for entire families to convert as a unit, in more recent times, particularly after the Communist revolution in the early 1970s, more and more young men who left their villages and lived among Christians in the city decided to convert. There was then a strong probability that his family would follow suit. This was especially true, related the interviewees, in cases when the contact between them would be severed if they did not convert.

It seems that Beta Israel's fear of the finality of whole families moving to Christianity encouraged family members who remained Jews to maintain fairly close ties with converts.[7] The Beta Israel recall without the slightest tinge of embarrassment that converts often lived close to their families and continued to visit them and even eat with them, so long as they maintained a strict separation of the slaughtering, preparation, and eating of meat.

A man from Gondar:

> Some who converted had families who didn't allow them in. There were some who were strict but others not so. Say someone's son went to the city, stopped observing Sabbath, ate nonkosher meat (that is, meat slaughtered by non-Jews), and all that. So for them he was gone, and they mourned him as though he had gone. They didn't really mourn for him like a dead person, but in their head. When someone is far from his home, doesn't accept their authority, doesn't marry a Jewish girl, then it's very painful for them. But on the other hand, if he comes to visit there are families who would ask him to go immerse himself in the river, wash his clothes, and if he does that they take him in. It's a compromise. When he just arrives they tell him, "Wait outside." But if he immersed himself and washes his clothes, he can come into the house and also into the synagogue. That's how it was for us. I think in more distant villages they were stricter.

And in another account:

> Those [who converted to Christianity] would come to visit their families in the village, but they couldn't come into the synagogue. If he came for a visit he could enter the house without immersing himself in the river, but not the synagogue. He wouldn't try to enter the synagogue anyway. If his parents are cooking meat for dinner he absolutely would not eat. If he went [converted], he went, and if there's a party or a celebration they let him slaughter for himself and then he can eat.

Most Jews wanted to view their relatives' conversion as a temporary lapse and accordingly permitted them to enter the house, if not the house of prayer, after a ritual ablution. Nonetheless, according to the interviewees' memory, many converts continued to participate in other holidays, and particularly in the Sigd[8] festivities, which, as already mentioned, attracted many Christians as well. The converts' continuous participation in these festivities was recalled by a Jew from the Gondar region:

> During the Sigd the converts would come as well. They would come back to the faith, to where their hearts were. And to vow. That's why a convert, if he has a family or relative or someone he wants to see because he misses them, he can see them all at the Sigd. It's a very big event. It's a meeting. Except for the prayers, it's the coming together, the kissing, seeing everyone, that's the important part. They would come to the Sigd and we would let them eat alone. *Felasmura* [another name for converted Jews] don't eat our slaughtering. So what do they do? We give them a sheep or two, depending on the number of people. They do eat *injera* [bread] and drink *tella* [beer] with us.

In coping with conversion, group commitment was perceived as essentially ethnic and therefore as primary and more powerful than the new religious-doctrinal commitment. The Jews spoke of converts who, in times of trouble, maintained their identification with Beta Israel—and particularly with their family and the people in their villages—as their emotional center of gravity. One such case was described by an immigrant from Tigre who distinguished between two types of converts:

> I knew a lot of people who converted. There was one Jew from our village who converted to Christianity. Afterwards he became rich and it bothered the Christians so they came to his house and took his son. So he came to us and asked us to help him. We took a group of people with weapons and went to the Christians and said, "Release the boy." The Christians were afraid and released him. [I asked:] So that convert returned to the Jews? [He answered:] No, he stayed with the Christians.

The same speaker also described the reverse situation. A Jewish priest from Wogera fell under the influence of the local Protestant mission and converted. After his conversion he cooperated with the mission and went from village to village preaching the gospel to the Jews.[9] This provoked a great deal of anger among the Jews but did not prevent them from meeting with him and discussing religious and other issues. Still, the speaker emphasized that had that *qes* wanted to return to Judaism, his betrayal of his descent would not have allowed the other *qesim* to perform the reconversion.

The attitude toward converts was influenced by their status and the

circumstances that led them to take the step. In the first example, the lay-
man was viewed as having converted due to his difficult lot. Thus, despite his conversion, he was considered a Jew who had converted un-
willingly. The story, which I heard as a first-hand account, relates that
this was made manifest when his son was in danger. He turned to the
members of his old religion, and they set out to help him against the Christians, his current "official" reference group, which had kidnapped his
son. Such a case stimulated a great deal of sympathy. But if a *qes* converted, betraying his sacred commitment to strengthening his religious
faith and his duty to support his people, this could no longer be forgiven.

The whole issue of conversion—its motivation, the lives of the converts, ongoing relations with them—is fraught with ambivalence. In many
cases, family and group commitments were maintained, but other cases
caused deep anger and mistrust. Some Jews were condescending, describing the convert as having been taken in by promises of a better life.
Others viewed the same convert as an opportunist who had decided to
slink back to Judaism as soon as he'd realized he was not going to get
what he had been promised. Similar considerations inform the present
debate about allowing "repentant" converts to immigrate to Israel as
Jews. One informant from the Gondar region noted:

> Those who went didn't want to remain Falasha. They just wanted to go fur-
> ther and further. But now, since the time of the State of Israel, they feel dif-
> ferent. Even now they still hope to immigrate to Israel. When the Jewish
> Agency established schools in the Gondar region, there was a big meeting and
> many suggested a return to the source. A few opposed the idea, saying that
> after so many years of being in Christianity it would make them unstable to
> return to the source when they were old. We [the Beta Israel] said that we are
> willing to accept them, and in the end they decided to send their children to
> the Jewish Agency schools. Look, from the start they didn't embrace Chris-
> tianity out of religious belief, only to improve their lot in life. It was only a
> material decision, not because they had studied and considered the matter.

FLESH, HEART, AND THE TWICE-DISGUISED HYENA

Many informants emphasized that even converts who were putatively
accepted into the Christian society while alive were barred from burial
in Christian cemeteries after death:

> They [the Christians] try to convince us and we say no! . . . They told us that
> if we come to them they'll give us money and there'll be land. They try to
> persuade us: "Believe in the *Wongel* [the New Testament]! It is the truth."
> So whoever wants money goes. He goes because he believes he'll have money

and land, and that's the way it is for a short while, but then they don't accept him. . . . Listen, in addition, if he dies, the Christians won't bury him in their grave. Just like I'm telling you. In the end, they don't bury Jews in their cemeteries.

Cemeteries mark the boundaries separating groups, manifesting both the ethnic and the religious affiliation of the dead. The cemetery is the place set on earth where members of a religious group are gathered and from which their souls ascend to heaven.[10] Thus, the informants see the exiling of the convert as proof that they are not viewed as full Christians: Even though they have undergone baptism, this cannot "change their heart."

Another aspect of this perception as portrayed by the Beta Israel was expressed in the suspicious and hostile attitude of the Christians, who continued to attribute supernatural powers to the converts.[11] In fact, the informants claimed that these suspicions became even more severe after a Jew's conversion:

The Christians still suspect them of eating people's flesh. They think that maybe the converts are worse than those who stayed in their own religion, because those who remained in their own religion are known, so their destructive power doesn't work if you're careful and watch them. But those who are in their midst still have that power and they're more dangerous. The Christians claim this.

In the eyes of the Christians, as the Jews understand it, their supernatural powers do not disappear when they "disguise themselves" as Christians. Clearly, the conversion doesn't change the innate ethnic essence. Their "disguise" only makes it more difficult to identify them. A Jew is still a hyena, the *buda*. His Christian identity is merely a better camouflage for his nocturnal operations. He is *doubly disguised* and *doubly dangerous*.

CHAPTER 8

Flesh and Bones

Jewish Masters, Jewish Slaves

I started interviewing the Beta Israel in 1985. As the months passed I felt that I had mastered the material enough to be able to anticipate what would come next. My interviewees also appeared increasingly comfortable with me. Had I not been disarmed by my feeling of easy mastery, I might have captured something startling. I would have realized that I had not understood what some of my interviewees had been saying inadvertently. They frequently used the term *barya*, a term they contrasted with the word *chewa*. *Barya* were somehow different from *chewa*. The Beta Israel were *chewa*, but some of the people living with them were *barya*.

An old lady frequently served us coffee while we talked, never said anything to me, and was rarely spoken to or noticed by my hosts. We had never been introduced and I wondered who she was. One day I dared to ask. It was as if they hadn't heard me. I tried again. Again they were "deaf." I understood after the second failure that for whatever reason, I would not receive a direct answer. Unexpectedly, the revelation came. The "invisible" old lady was a *barya*.

They had been talking about *barya* for months. A moment of casual conversation suddenly made the referent shockingly clear. The word *barya* meant "slave." The Beta Israel, the *chewa*, owned slaves.[1] One of them had been a silent presence with us for months.

My shock was twofold: I was astonished to realize not only that the Beta Israel owned slaves but that I had been listening for many weeks to their open acknowledgment of this fact without realizing what they had actually been saying. This revelation shook my faith in my mastery of the "story." What else had I been told that I had not heard? I knew now that if I pressed, they would become silent, evasive. If I appeared to become moralistic, I would endanger my whole enterprise. Rather than risk that danger, I decided to respect the limits they themselves had placed on the subject. Whatever went beyond those limits was to be kept secret. What they wanted to stress was the relation of slavery to the maintenance of group boundaries and their faithfulness to the religious doctrine which legitimized slavery.

This chapter reflects these limitations. But I knew that I would have to venture into this realm of secrets and attempt a more comprehensive exploration in my next study.

THE SLAVE AS A STRANGER

Cut off from Ethiopian society, severed from humanity in general—these are the prominent images that appear in Beta Israel depictions of the otherness of the *barya*. No one admitted to knowing where these slaves had originated. Though the people I interviewed could sometimes recall the slave markets, the precise origin and history of the slaves were presented in extremely vague terms. Some informants mentioned black Africa, by which they meant not a geographical entity but a symbolic concept representing "primitive," "wild Africa," standing in opposition to Ethiopia. Others conjectured southern Ethiopia, characterizing the region as wild and uncivilized, where someone might have "stolen" people during the night to sell them.[2]

I was told that the *barya* possessed no ancestral memory; that they were bereft of any knowledge of origin, completely cut off from their past: "He doesn't know who his mother is," or "He has nothing in his head from his parents."

For the Beta Israel, ancestral memory is a precious possession. Elders can reel off as many as seven or more generations of forefathers.[3] In such a society, lack of the most basic ancestral memory (one's father or mother), relegates one to a subhuman level. Parents teach a person how to be a human being. It was their parents who had taught them. To lack this ancestral source of information was to be other than human.

Religion, too, comes from one's ancestors. As a tabula rasa, this nonhuman being also lacked religion. Pagan animism was totally discounted as a religion. This, too, highlighted their otherness: "They have no faith, they believe in trees and stones, in nothing, just in some nonsense, in some tree or something."

Even after the slaves had undergone the conversion ritual, they continued to be perceived as less than human strangers: "He doesn't know how to pray, just says bo! bo! bo!"

During prayer, the narrative goes, the *barya* only groaned and grunted. It was like the inarticulate lowing of cattle. Despite the fact that the *barya* in most cases understood and spoke the language of his masters, his praying is described as nonhuman.

The impression of base otherness was reinforced by physical appearances. Beta Israel cited physical differences between themselves and the *barya* that would be indiscernible to an outside observer. Three physical attributes were cited: black skin color, frizzy hair, and dazzling white teeth. Black was the telltale sign of the tribe of Ham, whose affinity to black Africa made it less "civilized" than the red and more "civilized" descendants of the tribe of Shem. Frizzy hair was another sign of barbarism, being incapable of being tamed or controlled, combing it an impossible chore. Yet another distinction was externalized by teeth. White teeth, though described in a positive way—handsome and very strong— also served to associate the slave with wild, untamed Nature. Only in a primitive environment would such teeth be essential to survival. On many occasions I heard the following story:

> At the time of the flood, the days of Noah, Noah had three children: Shem, Ham, and Japheth. Noah was drunk and when he was drunk he stood without clothes. Ham saw him and laughed at him. Shem saw him and went behind him to dress him. When Noah woke up he blessed Shem that he should be a merchant and be rich and sell the *barya*. And to Ham he said, "You they will sell and buy." Ham was the father of the *barya*. The root of the *barya* went out from him.[4]

INITIATION RITES AND NAME GIVING

The interviewees considered it very important to emphasize that upon entering Beta Israel the pagan slaves underwent a ceremony of ritual conversion. Without it they could not have been admitted into Jewish homes. The conversion process was a watered-down version of the elaborate rituals of the Beta Israel,[5] without which one could not "use" the slave. He or she had to become a "Jew." The reigning attitude may be summed up by one informant's citation from Exodus 12:44, in relation to the paschal sacrifice: "But any slave a man has bought, may eat of it only if he has been circumcised." The *barya* themselves did not seek admittance into the group. The interviewees perceived conversion as vital for themselves, not for the slaves, as reflected in the shockingly unexceptional rationalization: "We did the ritual for them so that they could at least serve in the house. Look, if you bring a dog home you have to train it. You want it to be like you wish it. Even more so a person. At least he should behave like you do, and you want him to be loyal and all that, so you have to do the ritual."

The conversion process for male slaves included ritual circumcision.[6] Again, informants often cited the *Orit* (Exodus 4:25), explaining: "We live with the slave according to the *Orit*. Even though we buy him with money, we convert him and circumcise him. Zipporah, our teacher's wife, also performed circumcision."[7]

The process was not seen as difficult, painful, or even meaningful for the slaves. It was yet another demonstration of the religious devotion of Beta Israel.

In the final stage of the ceremony, the slaves were given names. Most of the names were peculiar to the *barya*, and denoted their bondage. Not infrequently, these names suggested a divine sanction for their enslavement.[8] Thus, the conversion ritual and the name-giving transformed the slave into a specifically Jewish *barya: barya Falasha*. In consequence of his or her new status, he or she was forbidden to marry a slave not of the Beta Israel.

SLAVES AND GROUP BOUNDARIES

A man from Tigre narrated:

> In Adiaro there was a Jew called Had'azgi Abraham, blessed be his memory. He lived exactly between a Christian and a Muslim, in the middle. One day there was a plague of locusts and the locusts ate only the crops of the Christians and the Muslims and didn't touch his, which were in the middle. When he went down to the market and everyone sat there to drink coffee the Christians and the Muslims were saying: God heard the Jews and did not harm them with locusts. And at the same time there was a *barya* of Israel that lived not far away and whose crops the locusts did eat. So the Christians asked (and laughed at us), "This is also a Jew, why did the locusts eat his?" As if they were saying to us: he's a slave, why do you make him a Jew? So we answered, "It is written in the *Orit* that when you buy him [the slave] make him a Jew. It is written in the book of Exodus chapter twelve, verses forty-four and onwards."

Beta Israel's denigration of the slaves and their religious status are evident here. The locusts harmed the converted *barya*'s crops but not those of the Jew Had'azgi. When taunted about the conversion of the *barya*, the Jews simply replied that such was the Biblical command, but that the conversion ceremony did not really make the leopard lose his spots. The *barya*, despite his conversion, had not become a "real Jew." The story thus betrays Jewish sympathy for the sentiment underlying the Christians' disparaging remark.

This same ambivalence arose regularly when the Beta Israel spoke about their slaves. References to the *barya* invariably evoked an excursion into questions of religious practice, focusing on marital relations and procreation, houses of prayer, ritual slaughter and dietary laws, and burial tensions. These subjects provided a framework for teasing out the dialectic of Judaism as a chosen faith and practice and as a nonnegotiable lineal descent and for exploring basic questions of religious boundaries and identity. *Barya* and *chewa* were absolutely forbidden to intermarry. The interviewees also took care to emphasize to me that slaves of the three religious groups (the "*barya*-Falasha," "*barya*-Christian," and "*barya*-Islam") could not contract marriages with each other. This interdiction was defended on religious grounds: "If one was the *barya* of a Jew, and his brother [meaning "group brother"] was the *barya* of a Christian, it is not important for us [that they are both *barya*], because although he was his brother, each one was in a different religion. The *barya* of a Jew was a Jew, the *barya* of a Christian was a Christian, and Muslim, Muslim."

Thus, while slaves were ethnic "brothers," affiliation to different religious groups precluded marriage between them. The interviewees made clear in discussion with me that institutionalized marriages could only be cemented between *barya* of the same religious group. Although this prohibition may feasibly be regarded as an attempt to safeguard the property of the group, Beta Israel presented their case in terms of a religious fait accompli: "Now he was already a Jew so there was no way he could marry a non-Jew."

The rigors of religious rules notwithstanding, marriage between *barya* partners, at least as evidenced from *chewa* testimony, was rather infrequent. There were economic problems. With which owner would the new couple live? Who would own their labor? Who would own their children? All of these problems were resolved by a simple expedient: informal liaisons between male masters and female slaves. A fringe benefit of these liaisons was the children they engendered. They became the property of the *barya*'s mother's master. The number of offsprings indicated both economic and sexual virility. The free status of the father did not descend to his mixed progeny. The smallest drop of *barya* blood would make the infant a *barya*. Only after many generations could the taint be diluted to the point that the beneficiary could marry a somewhat dé-classé *chewa*. Religious doctrine legitimized this practice; indeed, one informant quoted a historical precedent: "Jacob had many children. Levi, Shimon, Judah, and Issachar are Leah's children. Dan and Naphtali are Bilhah's who was her *barya*. Rachel's *barya,* whose name was Zilpah, bore four children; their mother was a *barya* and their father a *chewa,* Israel."

I had the feeling that the Beta Israel, in stressing the strict separation of blood lines between *barya* and *chewa* were trying to give me and other Jewish Israelis a warning against careless miscegenation.[9] The meticulous attention which Beta Israel devote to genealogical categories is sustained by a more basic distinction between flesh and bones. Even when the *barya* submitted to conversion, their "bones," in the words of the interviewees, were still *barya* bones. In other words, their "flesh" may have been converted, so to speak, but their bones remained *barya.* Over the generations, an increasingly complicated intricate hierarchy of mixed *barya-chewa* progeny emerged, matched by an equally intricate system of personal accounting.[10] The detailed genealogy of the slaves meshed well with accepted patterns of kinship, which relied on very deep ancestral memory.

A symbolic segregation from the core of Beta Israel society is most vividly seen in the restrictions placed on *barya* access to key religious institutions. The interviewees related that the *barya* were granted only restricted access to the house of prayer, and then only to specifically designated sections. This selectivity varied from region to region. In some locales, acccording to the interviews, the *barya* were not admitted into the house of prayer at all but only into its outer yard. For the most part, however, once the conversion ritual had taken place, they were granted limited access. At times, the restrictions were temporal:

> In our *masgid* [house of prayer] there was a difference with the *barya* . . . although converted he was allowed to enter only after three years. In this time we examined his heart to see what he thought, we didn't let him go in at once. If he had converted yesterday they didn't let him go into the synagogue. You had to wait a bit. Afterwards if he wanted to go in, he had to come with his master. Look, maybe I bought him today and tomorrow I'll sell him.

Another informant mentioned that the *barya* had permission to enter the house of prayer but was not permitted to remain there during the reading of the sacred *Orit*. Other informants stressed the spatial dimension of the restriction: "If a *barya* came into the *masgid* he sat there on the side . . . we wouldn't let the *barya* really enter the room of the *masgid*, only stand outside. A woman could come into a special place, not in the men's place, and the *barya* would stand outside the door. We wouldn't see him."

In the very detailed accounts on the subject, it appeared to be crucial for interviewees to emphasize the particulars of everyday practices concerning life with the *barya*. Only free men were allowed to stand alongside the holy books. Women stood at a distance over on the other side opposite the men; the *barya* were positioned behind the women.

Ritual slaughter and dietary laws made up yet another area of religious practice in which questions of religious identity and boundaries played out. As noted earlier, in the regions of Ethiopia in which the Beta Israel dwelt, each group ritually slaughtered the meat for its own consumption.[11] Additionally, within each group there was a hierarchy of who could slaughter for whom.[12] It was repeatedly emphasized that an animal slaughtered by a slave would not be fit for Beta Israel. A *barya* might eat of an animal slaughtered by Beta Israel, but not vice versa. Stories were told of a *barya* who went hunting for "kosher"[13] prey only to find that no one would touch his kill, even when the animal was ritually permitted. Other stories mentioned the hunting of animals by a *barya* for *barya* consumption alone.

Thus, it seems, the realm of ritual slaughter was dominated by perceptions of hierarchical order. Interviewees stressed during our discussions that a person might partake of meat only when slaughtered by someone of a higher religious status. Such is our own case: though the *barya* were located within the religious framework of the Beta Israel, they were relegated to its nethermost level. Even if the *barya* performed the slaughter according to all the minutiae of Jewish law, the meat would be considered ritually unfit for Beta Israel. The *barya* was not of the pure seed of Abraham. He could not perform ritually permitted slaughter for any but his own group.

Scarcely less meticulous than the rules controlling *barya* access to the house of prayer as described to me were rules restricting burial. Informants expressed a full gamut of opinions. While there were those who buried the *barya* in the Jewish cemetery like any Jew, others argued that the slave could be buried indiscriminately, in an open field or even in a place not specifically designated for burial.

Most of the interviewees spoke of various intermediate arrangements customary in their native parts of Ethiopia. As one informant related:

"When a *barya* died, they would bury him together with everyone else in the cemetery but they didn't perform the *maswa'it* ceremony or *tazkar* [rituals and prayers for the soul of the deceased] for him."[14]

Another speaker earnestly made clear his memory that in his native village they used to bury the *barya* near the cemetery, though not within its actual boundaries. Fundamental to such arrangements was the perception of the slave as "not a real Jew." Though the *chewa* concede that the *barya* was a Jew and worthy of a Jewish burial, his cosmological rank decreed otherwise. This point is related to the perception by which a slave retained *barya* "bones" even after conversion had rendered his "flesh" Jewish. With death, flesh decomposed; only the bones remained.

RELIGION AS FULCRUM

It may be recalled that Jewish converts to Christianity still retained—in the perception of Beta Israel interviewees—their essential Jewishness: "In their heart they are still Jews." Their new Christian "flesh" covered a heart that was unchanged. Likewise, the forced conversion of the *barya* to Judaism left their *barya* bones unchanged. The dialectic between inner and outer, shallow and deeper, "flesh" and "bones," was pervasive and immutable. Converted though he was, he and his offspring remained *barya*. But these ironclad distinctions were drawn within a wider context. The seemingly intrafamilial drama was pointedly addressed to a far more significant audience of Christians, and thus the attitudes toward the *barya* served as a touchstone for the Jews' own religious fastidiousness.

It might be useful to recall the specific ways in which the Jews portray Christian stigmatization of the Beta Israel in word and deed: Beta Israel were denied ownership of land. They were confined largely to denigrated occupations, they were accused of practicing magic, and, even though some Christians granted them a common ancestry, many others relegated their origin to an ancient, despised, pagan group known as Agaw. The Jews articulated their sense of the differences between themselves and their *barya* in precisely the same parameters. Of all the topics raised by the informants, those evoking the most heated responses concerned *barya* entry into the house of prayer or his burial in the Jewish cemetery. The Jews' avoidance of Christian houses of prayer and cemeteries was indeed central in delimiting religious groups throughout the area. A member of the Beta Israel would not enter a Christian church or a Muslim mosque, and at times would even take care to avert his eyes from them. A non-Jewish person would not be permitted to enter a Jewish house of prayer. By the same token, the cemeteries also constituted well-defined boundaries between religious groups in Ethiopia. Like the house of prayer, the cemetery was perceived as a site expressive of the religious communality of those buried within. Unlike the house of prayer, however, Christians were indeed permitted to enter a Jewish cemetery for practical purposes, such as bearing the dead, but the Beta Israel would never enter a Christian or Muslim cemetery. The cemetery was perceived as the last place on earth in which the Beta Israel congregated in toto. It was the place from which the yearning souls of the faithful would attempt to rise toward Heaven.

Determined to remain faithful to the commandment to reject all "other gods," the Beta Israel elected to justify their relations with the *barya,* still considered by the *chewa* to be essentially pagans, in a religiously acceptable manner. People I spoke with stressed that despite their closeness and interaction with the *barya,* their Jewishness was never compromised. The *barya* were converted, and Beta Israel purity was preserved. The tendency to frame relations with the *barya* in religious terms indicates the determination of the Beta Israel to render religious criteria the legitimate and abiding markers of intergroup boundaries. In the spheres of both praxis and cosmology, the perceptions of the circumscribed domain of slavery were dominated by a more fundamental agenda. There was one realm in which Beta Israel, everywhere oppressed, patronized, and denigrated by their Christian neighbors, could proclaim and prove their superiority, in a way that even their oppressors had to acknowledge. That realm was religion. Religion was the fulcrum with which they could lift the burdens imposed on their souls and raise their tragedy to a higher spiritual plane. Even their slaves, as oppressed by them as they had been by the Christians, served this agenda.

CHAPTER 9

Crucifiers and Idol Makers

Judaism and Christianity in the Village Square

In Ethiopia, everybody loves to argue. The inhabitants regard disputation as a form of entertainment.[1] Indeed, the lives of the Jews in Ethiopia are rife with disputes of a random, daily nature, as well as structured, more "official" debates. The verbal dispute dramatized the direct, explicit rivalry between Judaism and Christianity in Ethiopia in general, and between neighbors of the two groups in particular. Beta Israel immigrants recall many such debates. It is clear from their accounts that they aroused strong feelings on all sides: interviewees were still affected by the emotion triggered by these now-distant events. The claims of the two sides, as acted out before me, punctuated by dramatic gestures and loud voices, deviated from the usual equanimity of the interview.

Religious differences generated a persistent undercurrent in Ethiopian daily life. Earlier accounts in Protestant missionary literature[2] introduced the religious arguments used by the missionaries to discredit the most important religious rites and customs observed by Beta Israel.[3] Sacrifice was a special target for attack, with missionaries claiming that sacrifice contradicted the teachings of the Old Testament itself. This reasoning was used in the hope of persuading Jews that the New Testament—and hence Christianity—was the sole perpetuation of the true belief.

One documented dispute, of great renown both in the written testimony and in the memory of the group, took place in the court of Emperor Téwodros II (reigned 1855–1868). In 1862, a group of Beta Israel religious leaders was invited to appear in a public debate opposite Christian missionaries. The dispute focused on the issue of unity versus division in the divine nature.[4] This fiercely divisive issue was still explosive in daily arguments between the believers.

This chapter addresses the daily religious debates through the voices and interpretations of Beta Israel interviewees; the Christians of Ethiopia might, of course, have understood the issues very differently.

HAYMANOT DISPUTES

The term *haymanot* arose frequently in descriptions of these arguments. *Haymanot* means "faith" and refers to the totality of the beliefs and practices of any religious tradition.

Though the manifold inequality of the Jews' living situation occasionally expressed itself in the interviews, their deprived status was never an open or acknowledged issue in competitive debates. Competition came to the fore in the *haymanot* disputes.[5]

In our conversations, great emphasis was placed and much energy invested in these disputes. The Christians were far less inflamed in similar polemics with Muslims, who constituted a far larger cohort of the population. Ethiopian Jews expressed great pride in the contrast between their fractional status in the population and the vast intellectual energy that the Christians invested in confrontation with them. Thus, although daily contact between the groups was frequently laden with dangerous tension, *haymanot* was an accepted vehicle for disputation.

This study sees religion within the cultural context of its subjects, as a *master key idiom*,[6] anchored and networked into the many aspects of everyday life—family and kinship, purity and impurity, communal relations, and so forth. Religious idiom, in this case *haymanot,* dramatizes human interaction in profoundly moving terms, illustrating the interpenetration of religious concerns and the routines of particular individuals. Indeed, the epistemological implications are no less imperative: they provide the code.

Given the similarity between Jews and Christians in physical, linguistic, and other "skin-deep" cultural manners, religion was conceived as a deep differentiating factor between people from birth. A dynamic, transformative dialectic was maintained between differential religious affiliation and ethnic similarity. Cosmological-metaphysical arguments were dominated by this dialectic and provide a key for unlocking its puzzles.

The tension emerging from these daily battles was further heightened by the fact that Jews and Christians both related their identity to fixed written doctrines. Each religion commanded its own "correct" ritual observances. These dogmas established both the boundaries which divided them and the identifications which bound them.[7] The typical dispute was not only about the essence of this or that religion but about the rules of daily life as scripted by written doctrine. The dispute raised the awareness of affinities as well as differences, highlighting and strengthening both.

VERBAL CONFRONTATION

Daily confrontations arose in the course of working together in the fields or in the marketplace. These situations frequently invited disputes over the "right" thing to do. The confrontations were not prearranged. Sometimes, even a minor disagreement could trigger a spontaneous religious clash. In addition to random disputes, there were also prearranged encounters of rival religious leaders. Jewish and Christian priests would meet to pose religious challenges to one another. These encounters exhibited a more "elevated" polemical tone than the arguments between common people, which often turned into dangerously heated confrontations. The Jewish priests, especially those in high positions, also esteemed by the Christians as authorities on the Old Testament, were sought-after partners in debates.

Visually, the encounter took on the appearance of a public spectacle— religious theater. The rival priests were physically separated from each other and from the audience; thus secluded, they pored over their books. Despite the physical barrier, their similarities were evident. Both wore the same garb and white turban, designating them as clergy and distinguishing them from laymen. A prominent feature of the encounter was Ge'ez, the scriptural language of both Jews and Christians in Ethiopia, a language understood by religious figures but not by commoners.

The testimony of the participating qesim included that of my friend, qes Avraham, who, it will be recalled, was extremely eager to meet clergy of the Ethiopian Orthodox church in Jerusalem. Priests of both groups possessed knowledge of the doctrine of the other group, which, though perceived by the other as "selective" and "slanted," was quite thorough. Scripture served to focus the discussion, which was conducted in a calm, tolerant, even affable atmosphere. Most of the religious figures I interviewed confessed that they longed for those disputes and missed them sorely now that they lived in Israel. They had provided a stage for the display of religious sophistication, created a feeling of closeness, and despite a show of equality, confirmed an inner superiority over their counterparts on the Christian side.

Speakers claimed that Christian *qesim* instigated more encounters than did Jews. They would send someone to arrange a meeting with one or more Jewish priests, who would agree and wait at the appointed spot. Whether the meeting took place outdoors in the village square or in the home of one of the priests, the two sides kept physically apart. A Jew from Ambober told of frequent meetings between his grandfather, a renowned and respected *qes,* and a Christian *qes.* The encounters would take place in the village square, with a stone fence built by his grandfather, separating the rival *qesim.* This type of barrier was mentioned in other accounts. This was the wish of the Jewish priest, recounted his grandson, and the condition was accepted by the Christian priest, who cooperated in order to adapt to the distancing requirements of Beta Israel.

The encounters were typically accompanied by interpretations and translations of Ge'ez. Beta Israel chose to present this as indication of the clear reliance of the Christian clergy on the knowledge possessed by the Jewish religious figures. The greater expertise in this language was construed as a sign of more profound religious knowledge. In the example cited above, the converted *qes* was trying to persuade the Jews of the truth of Christianity. During the public discussion, the Jewish priest introduced expressions in Ge'ez, and the convert, nonplused, fell into the trap and displayed his fatal ignorance of the sacred language, revealing to all, as construed today in the interviewees' memories, the "superficiality" of his religious lore.

A debate by its very nature must convey at least a momentary semblance of equality. Fair competition occurs between parties on an equal footing in a physical and social space aimed at guaranteeing relative neutrality. The religious dispute between clergy also radiated an atmosphere of spiritual elation. In contrast, the arguments between the common people exhibited more of the vulgarity and inequality of the daily reality lived by Jews among Christians in Ethiopia.

WHAT WAS THE DISPUTE ABOUT?

The disputes made no clear-cut distinction between cosmological issues and conduct. Behavior was seen as deriving from one's religious culture. Disputes over *haymanot* were arguments about the necessary internal connection between the groups' religious culture and conduct. Conduct was of compelling interest to the participants, raising strong emotions—even stronger than issues of religious ideology as such. For example, Jewish dogma forbids the eating of bloody meat. The spectacle of Christians gorging themselves on blood-drenched meat was physically nauseating to the Beta Israel.

From a structural point of view, virtually every dispute covered a number of major debating points that recurred in a more or less fixed sequence:

1. Whose religious doctrine is legitimate?
2. Is Jesus divine?
3. Who crucified Jesus?
4. How should blood and the shedding of blood be dealt with?

WHOSE RELIGIOUS DOCTRINE IS LEGITIMATE?

One way through which the status of Judaism was frequently debated was to claim the superiority of each group's scripture: "We are not arguing, the book is speaking. . . . We would argue which of the books was better. They say *Wangel* [the New Testament] is big, and we say the Torah is big."

The Beta Israel identify very strongly with the Torah—the *Orit*. When they invoke the superiority of the Torah, they thus feel that they are on very solid ground.

The New Testament, as they see it, is blatantly false, since, they believe, it was written by a human hand: "We tell them, what is *Wangel?* They took a little from the Torah, a little from the Muslims, a little from here and a little from there. We received only from God. We received the Torah from God. What would the Christian answer us? They would only say: Christ, and that's all. First it was yours, now it is ours. That's what they keep saying."

Both groups supported the claim that scripture originated with the Jews. The difference was in the way each used the contention to its own advantage: the Christians taking pride in having adopted the revised and most current text, and the Jews emphasizing their preferred status as original inheritors.

A man from the Tigre region developed this point:

There was always arguing between us. The Jews always said "We are your fathers," and the Christians also believed that. In the Tigre area we're not so far [apart]. But they said that a new law came out and we [the Jews] didn't accept it, so the Christians would say: "We accepted the first law and the second one too, but you remained with the first." . . . We always told the Christians: "The world began with the Torah and will end with the Torah."

These examples reflect a determination to portray the New Testament as lacking in sacred value, written by a human, not a divine hand—and not presented by God to his own people. The Christians do not question that the Torah was divinely written, but they believe that the only sacred writing now valid is the New Testament, which replaced the Old. Accepting the sacred status of the Torah does not, they say, diminish the sacred status of the New Testament. The Christians still value the Jews as "the people of the book"—but the book itself has been replaced by a new, improved edition.

Unlike the New Testament, the Quran was regarded as a book that posed no threat to the Torah.[8] As the Jews read it, the Quran contained no significant addition to the *Orit*. Indeed, many interviewees considered the Quran basically similar to the Torah, though written in a different language.

The Beta Israel believed that they had no fundamental arguments with the Quran. The fact that it was written in a different language from the *Orit* insulated this conviction from easy refutation. At the same time, the rivalry between the Old and New Testaments was highlighted and intensified by their common language. The Jews prided themselves on what they conceived was their mastery of Ge'ez. A perennial undertone of arguments over substance was the competition over subtleties of exegesis.

From the time of Italian rule in Ethiopia (1936–1941), the *Orit* and the *Wangel* were printed together in a single volume, known as *mes'haf qeddus,* the Holy Book. Such volumes were printed both by Protestant missionaries and by the Ethiopian Church and distributed without charge or sold for a small sum. In the absence of other editions of Scripture, these books served both religious communities. Though the Jews used this edition and in certain places even brought it into the synagogue, the Jewish priests would tear out the pages of the New Testament from the book. Beta Israel stressed that the fact that the Christians printed the two tomes together proved that they not only recognized the importance of the Old Testament but depended upon it as foundation of their faith. In the course of the disputes, the Jews emphasized that the Christian clergy could not manage without the *Orit*, whereas the Jews, for their part, had no need or use for the New Testament. The Jewish rejection of the New

Testament as a sacred text and a design for living mandates a cognate rejection of Christians as a divinely guided people.

According to the Beta Israel, their ancestors possessed books that they brought with them from the Holy Land when they arrived in Ethiopia. These "original" Jewish books, they believed, were appropriated by the Christians, who hid them in their churches. After the Christians took all the original parchment manuscripts, they had them printed and circulated among the Jews as well. In these accounts, the Christians wrested the Torah, which is Judaism itself, from the Jews by force, then returned it to them in a different (printed) version, while the Christians continued to hold on to the original handwritten scrolls: "They took it and printed it all by machine and gave it to us. Now they know everything and now they're saying, 'All this is ours,' but ours is the real Torah itself, they took it and put it into their *mes'haf qeddus.*"

In the words of another interviewee: "Our Torah has for a long time been in *their hands.*"

These alleged acts inspire a great deal of frustration and anger, rising to condemnation of the attitude shown by Christians to Judaism and to the Beta Israel. The frustration was more marked in the historical story than in contemporary disputation. Perhaps the greater "factual" distance of the historical expropriation made the anger and condemnation less dangerous to express.

IS JESUS DIVINE?

Aside from issues of doctrine and legitimacy discussed in the disputes, each group would also cite references from the Holy Book of the rival group.

The question of the divine nature of Jesus and his crucifixion figured prominently in the disputes. For their part, Beta Israel drew upon classical internal Christian polemics, thereby raising issues used by opponents of Christian monophysite doctrine, stressing a single divine essence, incarnated in the figure of Jesus.

The Jews thus would adduce proof from the New Testament, usually quoting Luke 2:48, in which Mary says to Jesus, who disappears and then reappears, on his way to Jerusalem: "Your father and I have been anxiously looking for You." The Beta Israel cited this verse as clear proof that Joseph, a man of flesh and blood (not the Holy Spirit), was the father of Jesus—and, like all human fathers, would worry about his missing son.

One account tells:

> We can argue whether Jesus was an angel who came from heaven, whether
> Mary his mother wasn't married and was a virgin, and whether he got into
> her just like that from the air and then was born. When they say he came first
> from heaven, we say to them: Jesus didn't come from heaven, he was born to
> his father Joseph. And it says that Jesus was a little boy and he ran away from
> home and his mother Mary said to him when he came back: "Where were
> you? Your father and I looked for you." So the Christians say she just "said"
> that and it doesn't mean anything. They didn't have sexual relations. And we
> said to them that Jesus is a regular man, just a regular man. We would argue
> about that a lot.

Trying to prove that the sacred book of Beta Israel contains a prophecy
of birth by a virgin, the Christians quoted the Old Testament: "Look,
the young woman is with child and about to give birth to a son. Let her
name him Immanuel" (Isaiah 7:14). This verse, as is well known, is frequently used by Christians in other cultural contexts to prove that the
birth of Jesus is prophesied in the Old Testament.

Another Old Testament reference cited in relation to the claim of Jesus' divine nature was the story of Abraham and the three angels (Genesis 18). The Christians quoted this to prove the possibility that the divine nature can be simultaneously present in additional figures.

The speakers sometimes included the following literary reference as
a "story within a story" when narrating the famous debate in front of
Téwodros II.

A qes from Tigre recounted:

> King Téwodoros invited the big chief priest of the Christians and a Jewish
> qes of ours and asked each one to bring his letter (Scripture). The Christian
> said: "Ours was born of the Holy Spirit." Then the Jew said: "But we have
> one God who created heaven and earth. He created the beginning and made
> man in his own image on the sixth day. For this reason we have one God."
> Then the Christian said: "You have three Gods who went in to Abraham's
> house." "It wasn't three Gods," replied the Jew. "It was only one God with
> three faces, their bodies were three but it is only one God," and he added:
> "That isn't God, those were angels that God sent to Abraham's house, they
> weren't God Himself."

The Christian effort to find proof of Jesus' divine nature in the Old
Testament and the Jewish attempt to find proof for their claims in the
New Testament highlight the fact that both groups shared the same fun-
damental concept of divinity and took this common ground for granted.

The question was not whose divinity was authentic, assuming competing divinities, but which people did the one and common divinity favor? Analysis of the specific claims raised in the disputes underscores this point and even goes beyond it. The religious disputes between Jews and Christians always took place against the backdrop of another ongoing rivalry, the one between the Ethiopian Church and the Protestants. In the debate over the essence of the divine nature, the three relevant groups—the Ethiopian Church, the Protestant missionaries and the Jews—all drew on arguments from both Old and New Testaments. Both the Jews and their Christian neighbors deployed debating points derived from the two great sources against the other groups.

Belief in Jesus' divinity is one proof of the superficiality of Christian faith, according to the Jews. In this context, Beta Israel called upon the Muslims. Like the Jews and unlike the Christians, the Muslims also believe in only one God, felt by the Jews for this selected purpose to be the same one that they believe in. Christians, however, have many god-figures, hence, their religion is weaker. This perception hints at pagan elements in the ways the Christians *express* their faith. There was almost no interview touching on this issue that did not mention worship of the divine figures in Christianity as proof of the polytheistic ways of the Christians.

As craftsmen working with metal and wood, Jews were requested to make and repair the Christian idols, metal crosses, and other articles of worship. In the eyes of the Jews, this cast them in the role of "idol makers" and brought home to them the distance between man-made gods and their own invisible God. The term "idol" was repeated in different contexts when the interviewees spoke of Christians: "We make Jesus and Mary and all the idols for them and then they pray to them."

And: "We would say to them, we are sitting on your god, your god is made of wood. If I sit on a wooden chair it's as if I'm sitting on him. I told them so myself."

The response of Beta Israel to the fact that the Christians "made God themselves," or even worse, required Jews to make the figures they prayed to, gave endless opportunity for subtle satire: "We would mock them, oh, you're so righteous. *Our God* made *us*. *You* make *your* God. You're so righteous."

Or, in the words of another interviewee: "We told them, you're so rich, you have many gods, and we only have one."

The seemingly light-hearted tone of this particular interchange does not diminish the underlying tension of grim seriousness that generally pervaded these debates.

WHO CRUCIFIED JESUS?

Another central point in the dispute arises from the blame that the Christians lay upon the Jews for killing Jesus. The historical-religious guilt and responsibility for killing Jesus is inextricably attached to Beta Israel's current religious practices. The blood guilt is hereditary and innate. Living Jews are considered descendants of the very same Jews who crucified Jesus. Evidence for this accusation of murder was found in the ritual slaughter and ritual sacrifice practiced by Beta Israel.

I have already discussed the unbroken connection the Christians made between the paschal sacrifice and the tragic sacrifice of Jesus. Likewise, the attitude of the Christian neighbors to the slaughter of animals on Friday prior to the Sabbath, as shaped in the memory of the Beta Israel, is recalled with great pain: "I remember they told us that it's as if we were killing Jesus all over again. When we slaughter a goat on Friday it's as if there is something in the Jewish blood that makes us kill a goat every Friday. They told us, because you killed Jesus on Friday, you do it today and every Friday. They told us that many times."

When recalling the actual practices associated with religious belief, members of both groups entered a state of emotional turmoil. Any action affecting the human body awakens stronger reactions than intellectual discussions of abstractions—provoking primordial repulsion and disgust among members of the two groups.

The interviewees recalled their attempts to respond to passionate accusations of killing Jesus as attempts to raise the discussion to a more rational level. Here, too, the New Testament was frequently quoted to strengthen their defense.

A common reply attacked the very claim that a divine being can be killed: "That's your God? How can you kill God?" This question conveyed an implied aspersion which had already been raised in different forms regarding Jesus' divinity, and this moved the discussion from praxis to cosmology, setting it in a wider, more comprehensive context. Another response which they recalled with pride as especially sophisticated drew upon the common knowledge that in the period that Jesus was crucified, all the Christians were in fact still Jews, and only after his death did the split occur. When Ethiopian Jews were accused by the Christians of killing their Christian Jesus, the Jews would reply that at the time *there were no Christians.* There was only one group: "We told them that we all had the same father at that time."

Jews who did acknowledge the act of the crucifixion denied culpability or connection with that event. One account said that any blame is to be laid at the door of the Romans, not the Jews. This approach is based upon sources in the New Testament. A typical rebuttal was: "Yes, the Jews are connected with the killing of Jesus, but it happened somewhere else, so we personally are not responsible."

Another controversy centered around the question of Jesus' own faith. Beta Israel presented Jesus as a believing Jew who observed the Sabbath. They cited the story of how Jesus did not leave his grave until the Sabbath was ended (Matthew 28:1), because he observed the Sabbath. From this, Beta Israel concluded that he observed the Jewish Sabbath as the day of rest.

As a consequence of the sin of killing Jesus, the Jews were punished, exiled from their land, and dispersed.[9] This served also to justify the exclusion of the Jews from land tenure: it is a punishment they merited "from heaven." In contrast, a benevolent God compensated the Christians with power and land. Against such accusations, the Jews would usually reply that God was testing them and that they—and not the Christians—would eventually return to Jerusalem. Indeed, when *qes* Avraham met with the Christian priest in Jerusalem, he confirmed triumphantly the ultimate victory of the Jews, pointing to their mass arrival in the Holy Land.

HOW SHOULD BLOOD AND THE SHEDDING OF BLOOD BE DEALT WITH?

Spirited daily disputes centered around customs relating to blood, or, more specifically, rules governing menstruation, ritual slaughter, and eating. Members of the two groups who chose to discuss these physical customs located the controversy over *haymanot,* the different medium by which each religion comprehends the connection between human and divine. Blood was a flash point and key symbol.

Disputes over blood marked a tension—to use the structuralist formulation—between the polarities of nature and culture. Exemplary were such bipolarities as purity and impurity, internal and external, and passages from life to death. Each religion endowed common physical manifestations with cosmological-religious significance. A dispute relating to the most basic physical aspects of human existence stressed the religious divide between the groups. The argument implicitly acknowledged the similarity of all human beings, as well as the existence of a single higher power, referred to as *egziabehar,* a term shared by the two groups to denote the same divinity. The dispute openly focused, then, on the medium, different in each religion, linking human beings to God.

TWO MODELS: THE "DEAD END" AND THE "ALTERNATIVE PATH"

Religious debates offered a mutually acceptable mode for explaining and mediating the tension between affinity and conflict. The religious idiom was the quintessential, significant, and legitimate mode for the explication of the relations between the two groups and the boundaries between them. It may be said, of course, that the disputes took place between individuals, not groups or group ideologies, and they also had concrete, mundane objectives, such as entertainment and persuasion.

Nevertheless, relations between the two groups were complex and full of contradictions. The strong bond each group had with its religious doctrine, as seen over and over in the disputes, as well as the affinity between the Old and New Testament doctrines, created a wealth of possibilities that could explain the daily relations between the groups and the inconsistent intergroup concepts of their members.

Clearly, different individuals recall different aspects of the religious debates, and individual emphases shape the varied topography of the memory landscape. All the memories, however, take shape vis-à-vis the Christian model of relations between God and the different religions. As such, they comprise an alternative model, and even when the same issue was repeated, it might receive different interpretations. The structure and content of these religious disputes, as well as what was absent from them, reveal a basic given for the interviewees, namely, that the Jews and their Christian neighbors believed fundamentally in "the same power," which each group addressed after its own fashion. In light of this belief, the religious disputes should be seen as attempts on the part of each group to define its place not only in relation to the rival group but in relation to the divine power in which both groups believed.

The central issues raised in the *haymanot* disputes, as I read them, show two alternative models representing the connections between Judaism and Christianity. In order to present the conceptual models of the *haymanot* as rivalry over the divine power, one might invoke the analogy of the competitive sport of running. Beta Israel claimed that Christianity was fundamentally different from Judaism in that it was false. Following the separate track model, they held that the Christians were on another track altogether—and it led to a dead end. The Christians, as the Jews understood it, employed a model that can be likened to a relay race, in which Christianity was the natural, legitimate continuation of Judaism. The Christians did not deny the holiness of the Old Testament but claimed that the New Testament and Christianity had replaced it.

CHAPTER 10

Our Blood, Their Blood

Menstruation, Slaughter, and Eating

Blood is a highly charged symbol in many cultures.[1] Both Judaism and Christianity grant it great doctrinal significance. It symbolizes the covenant between the believer and God, governed by many commandments and prohibitions.[2]

Ethiopian society brought Beta Israel into daily contact with blood in a religiously significant way. Since the meanings attached to blood were central both for the Christians and for the Beta Israel, blood became the major criterion for determining religious legitimacy, a battleground between different conceptions of the same symbol. In this battle both sides used the same weapons. Although the perceptions of Beta Israel are deeply ingrained in Ethiopian culture, there is a constant process of negotiation over the parameters of Beta Israel's existence as a separate group within the Christian milieu.

As a key symbol[3] for both groups, blood was an interface around which each group struggled to define its distinct identity. This primordial symbol was a focal point for communication and for the continual articulation of differences. When Beta Israel described modes of behavior and conceptions that pertained to blood, the description took cognizance of their neighbors' conceptions and praxis with regard to the same symbol. The two systems were understood to be opposed.

MENSTRUATION

Menstrual blood was a central topic in the daily exchange between neighbors from both groups. For the Jews, it determined the purity of the entire group. The authority was the Old Testament verse, "And if a woman have an issue, and her issue in her flesh be blood, she shall be seven days in her menstrual separation: and whoever touches her shall be unclean until evening" (Leviticus 15:19). It was quoted to me during the interviews when we discussed the separation of Jewish women during their "unclean" periods. In accordance with the *Orit* (Leviticus 12:2–6), Beta Israel also considered the postpartum period as impure (forty days if a boy was born, eighty for a girl). During these menstrual and postpartum periods, Beta Israel women were confined to separate huts situated at the periphery of the Jewish dwellings. A stone fence set the area off from the rest of the village, with several women sometimes occupying the hut together. Each month, a woman would retire for seven days to the house of blood, and on the evening at the end of the seventh day, she would purify herself in the river and return home. Although women sometimes cooked for themselves during this time in the house of blood, they generally received food from outside, served to them over the stone fence. The existence of houses of blood and the customary separation were so conspicuous that at times it was described as the central sign of the existence of Jews in a village.

Unlike the Jews, Ethiopian Christian women did not maintain any special form of separation during their menstrual period. Not considered impure at that time, she remained at home, cooked, and maintained contact with other people. The differences in the menstrual customs between Beta Israel and the Christians were, then, public and known to all.

The privacy which characterized the Christian treatment of menstrual blood, as opposed to the public character of Beta Israel's treatment, was the subject of much debate. There were Christians who argued that, although their wives remained at home during their monthly period, they refrained from sexual relations. In Jewish ritual, the female fertility cycle was given to public scrutiny and observation, whereas for the Christians this was a private matter. Beta Israel believed that by making the woman's menstruation publicly known, they could control the time of conception and thus ensure the purity of the next generation. The Jews claimed that the Christians could never trace the identity of the real father of a woman's children.

The attempt to control the purity of the next generation by following the monthly cycle was central to the way Beta Israel perceived themselves. In intergroup debates about the customs of ritual impurity, Beta Israel would provocatively argue against the Christians that "only when your mother is about to die will she reveal to you who your father is."[4]

The deep concern with the menstrual blood of the other group indi-

Figure 17. Jewish woman in the "blood hut," Walaqa, Ethiopia, 1984.
Photograph by Doron Bacher, courtesy of Beth Hatefutsoth Photo Archive.

cates a unique convergence of categories for determining ritual purity, as each group portrayed the other's practices through its own religious terms of reference. This sort of symbolic community between two competing religious groups is far from self-evident. Analysis of the data indicates that for the Beta Israel the two definitions of purity and impurity belong to the *same* symbolic and conceptual system.[5] The Christians' nonobservance of the menstrual laws is cited by the Beta Israel as one of the main reasons for avoiding physical contact with them and for not eating food cooked by Christians.

According to one woman: "During their menstrual period, the Christian women stay at home [and don't move into the house of blood like the Jewish women]. Can I say something? They say to us, how come when you Jewish women bleed you leave the house? That's really disgusting! So we tell them that we got that from our Torah, we can't stay home during our period. That's how it is with our tribe. Everyone in Ethiopia is with his own tribe."[6]

As one man explained: "Our women would spend seven days in the menstrual house, and on the seventh day they would immerse themselves. On that day they don't eat anything until evening. Christians don't care. They would say to us: Blood is a flower. What are you afraid of, it's flower blood. It's an *ababa* [flower]."

This citation by the Jew was accompanied by grimaces of revulsion. In another interview, a women said: "They would tell me, are you crazy to be in the house [of blood] alone all day and all night? Maybe a wild animal will come to catch you. So I told her: All this time a wild animal has never come. They guard us when we are there."

Each group's interpretation of the same physiological situation as reincarnated through Beta Israel's recollections was accompanied by similar feelings of revulsion at the other side's practices and symbolically summarized the relations between the groups. Although the Beta Israel and the Christians have separate customs of purity and impurity, both groups were preoccupied with the purity and impurity of the "other woman." These categories served as a basis for disputations, comparisons, and evaluations. The two groups appeared to be utterly different, with the different menstrual customs reinforcing boundaries between them.[7] Yet they judged each other by the same criteria in a way that bespeaks the unspoken idea that the two groups were part of one system.[8] Intergroup conceptions about ritual slaughter and eating were also part of this understanding.

SLAUGHTER

Meat is a central ingredient in the Ethiopian diet, and both its slaughter and its preparation are governed by communal custom. Beta Israel slaughter was undertaken meticulously and with utmost attention to the relevant Biblical prescriptions governing the covenant between God and the believers (Exodus 29). Slaughter was described in vivid terms and accompanied by many demonstrations of emotion. Jewish slaughter was performed with a razor-sharp knife, so the passage from life to death was as quick and painless as possible: "Our *qes* slaughtered very well. The knife was not touched by the blood. It remained as it was, it was so clean afterwards. . . . With the Jews the knife is so sharp that the cow doesn't even hear that they are slaughtering it."

On the other hand, Beta Israel described the Christian slaughter as the very opposite of their own. Their slaughter was "too slow" and therefore cruel; the Christians were depicted as people who ate meat from animals that were not slaughtered in accordance with careful and caring rules:[9] "The *goyim* [meaning Christians] don't care that it hurts the cow . . . the Christians will eat [meat] slaughtered by any one of them, even children and even slaves."

Although the Christians recite a blessing when slaughtering, their blessing was considered short and inappropriate in light of their "barbarian," "nonreligious" methods. The following description demonstrates the interviewee's meticulous acquaintance with Christian slaughter practices:

> But [giving] Jewish meat to a Christian, Christian to a Jew, Christian to a Muslim is forbidden. Because it's souls, right? The Muslims do *"bissimallah"* [in the name of Allah], right? The Christians do *"Basema ab wawald wamanfas qeddus ahadu amlak"* [in the name of the Father, the Son, and the Holy Spirit one God] and then slaughter. The Jews say *"Baruch yitbarek amlak yisrael"* [Blessed is the King (God) of Israel]. That is because the cow was in her life [alive], she had life, birds are the same, a hen was in its life so everyone does his own blessing. . . . In slaughtering there are differences, the Christians, even if they find a cow that is already dead, they would still eat her. If a cow fell down and died they would eat her. Even if she had died before. And also their knife isn't so good. We have a special knife just for slaughtering.

When asked how *Christians* felt about the Jew's slaughtering practices, the response was that the Christians likened Beta Israel's slaughter to the murder of Jesus. In Christianity, blood and the crucifixion of Jesus are intimately linked: Jesus' spilt blood is an indication that the Jews have transgressed the Old Testament prohibition against bloodshed. The blood of Christ is thus both a cause and a sign of the veracity of the new divine order.[10]

Jesus' blood is perceived as purifying, forgiving, and redeeming.[11] Being the progeny of Christ killers, the Beta Israel carry "in their blood" inherited traits of the murderers of God.[12] Beta Israel always slaughtered their animals outside, where all could see. The slaughtered animal was then hung on a tree in order to drain its blood. For the Christians, this act evoked Jesus' crucifixion on a cross of wood. In a similar way, as mentioned before, the Christians believed that the crucifixion was a Jewish paschal sacrifice, reenacted in the Beta Israel's Passover sacrifice.[13] The conceptual circle revealed here is based upon a mutual projection between a doctrine (the crucifixion of Jesus by the Jews) and a reaction to praxis (the paschal offering). One speaker claimed: "They [the Christians] always said to us: 'On Passover you take a lamb and hang it on a high tree and stab it, just like you Jews did to Jesus.'"

Each group is revolted by the slaughter customs of the other group, just as with the menstrual customs. The blood of the victim, which can, according to Judaism, strengthen the covenant between God and Jewish believers,[14] is viewed by the Christians as the blood on account of which the Jews were abandoned and a new covenant was established between God and the followers of Christ.

EATING

The third blood-related theme is "eating" or, more specifically, the different practices governing the consumption of meat. The diet of the different groups in the area where the Jews lived was similar, and the Beta Israel spoke of a complete identity with regard to everything involving food.

The one exception was meat. Animals were slaughtered and meat was handled differently by the two groups, each with its own rules governing cooking and eating. Beta Israel repeatedly expressed their revulsion at the Christian custom of leaving blood in the slaughtered animal and even eating the animal "raw," that is, still bloody.[15] The raw meat, they stated, carries many parasites that caused different kinds of diseases from which Beta Israel were free.

One man said: "Christians will eat raw meat, like dogs. We say to them, you are eating like dogs, that's not good. We laugh with them. They say to us: You don't know, it's very tasty. . . . We tell them that if they don't cook the meat they will have worms in their bellies."

In the Old Testament, there is an explicit prohibition against eating bloody meat and consuming blood in any way: "Therefore I said to the children of Israel, None of you shall eat blood. . . . For the life of all flesh is its blood, on which its life depends: therefore I said to the Children of Israel, you shall eat the blood of no manner of flesh: . . . whoever eats it shall be cut off" (Leviticus 17:12–14). For the Christians, however, human and animal blood was perceived in the context of Jesus' purifying blood, and the symbolic consumption of Jesus' blood is one of the observances that granted the believer entry into heaven. One often-repeated allegation made by the Beta Israel is that, while they themselves had not witnessed it, the Christians drank the blood of Jesus and in order to achieve eternal life, they might even drink the blood of Christianized Jews after the converts had died. One interviewee explained:

> The Christians have a law that they call *segaw wademu* ["his flesh and blood"]. It is written in their *Wangel* that whoever eats the blood, will go to heaven and will be forgiven for all his sins. So a little child or a man who wants to be a priest, they feed him blood . . . so we think that they take the converts,[16] they take their body and their limbs after they die.

It would seem that the Christians' consumption of raw meat was for the Jews concrete proof that there was truth in this story.

Thus the Christians are described by the Beta Israel as "blood eaters" who transgress one of the central edicts of the Torah, an edict linked in their understanding with culture and humanity in general.

On the other hand, the Christians' conception of the Beta Israel as *buda* is also linked, as described earlier, to "eating."[17] The accusation that Beta Israel were *buda,* with all it implies in terms of invoking supernatural forces, was the accusation of "eating": "They would accuse us of eating a Christian" in their night guise as hyenas. "The Jews dug up children's graves in order to drink the babies' blood."

Jews and Christians thus both accused each other of eating blood.[18] Beta Israel described the consumption of uncooked, bloody meat by the Christians, while the Christians claimed that Beta Israel possessed magical "eating" abilities. In both cases the sheer humanity of the other group was placed in doubt. This symbolic reciprocity was forcibly expressed in both the content and the phonetics of the following account: "The Christians would say to us that we are *jib,* a hyena, which eats people. So we would answer that they are *dib,* that is, a bear. Why? Because what does a bear eat? It eats raw meat, right? Maybe a mouse or something like that they [the bears] eat."

The boundaries between the groups were conceptually organized as a series of binary oppositions recurring on various levels. In one respect, blood was central to the relationship between the believer and God in both Judaism and Christianity. In the relations between the Beta Israel and their Christian neighbors blood became a distinctive symbol of identity, standing at the center of the complex relations between the two competing religious groups. When I examined Beta Israel's descriptions, I found that every time they described themselves, they gave a rich and detailed account of Christian behavior as well. These descriptions contained a surprising degree of emotional, symbolic, and conceptual similarity, organized symmetrically so that each group's customs were portrayed as the reflected shadow of the other's.

In another respect, the "choice" of blood as an identity symbol and group marker exemplifies the centrality of separation for Beta Israel. Their maintenance of menstrual customs, which are a condition for pure birth, of slaughter customs, which span the boundary between life and death, and of specific forms of "eating"—the activity which fortifies and maintains the body—distinguished them from their neighbors in a manner perceived as primordial, nonnegotiable, and impervious to persuasion. In these three realms there was a "crossing of borders"[19] on the physical, tangible level with blood bursting forth, thereby trespassing its natural, set boundary within the body. Finally there was a selective transferring of the symbolic to the social in the living relations between the two groups. While on the social level there were strictly enforced rules against trespassing, there was in fact much fluidity and actual passage between the groups, such as in intermarriage or conversion. This tension between manifest declarations and actual practices turned the border crossing typical of blood into a highly charged focal point.

The framework of binary oppositions linked to blood was thus constituted of oppositions conceived of as primordial and untraversable, while on another level the possibility of negotiation and even transformation was hinted at, threatening the rigidity of the group categories.

CHAPTER 11

The Battle of Metaphors

Fire and Water versus Clay Vessels

Proverbs are indispensable carriers of meaning. Combining narrative and "editorial" elements, mingling comedy and tragedy, praise and blame, they raise the commonplaces of daily life to the level of unquestioned wisdom. This chapter examines three proverbs that share a single metaphor based on the Amharic term *dohoné*,[1] a vessel made of mud mixed with straw. The Jews privately employ the term *dohoné* as an insulting code word referring to the Christians. The *dohoné* metaphor is accompanied by opposing concomitant metaphors representing the Jews. These contrasting metaphors are explicitly located or implicitly assumed in the proverbs, inasmuch as they are subsidiary to the metaphor of the *dohoné*.

The three proverbs were interwoven with interviewees' descriptions and explanations of the different "natures" of the Christians and the Jews in Ethiopia.

The exegetic potential of the Ethiopian *dohoné* metaphor accords with Brenda Beck's well-expressed observation: "A metaphor points to the existence of a given set of abstract relationships hidden within some immediately graspable images. . . . Anthropologists, like philosophers, have long debated the status of the 'world out there.' . . . The metaphor is one of the simplest and most important mechanisms by which such a shared mental framework (or culture) can be kept in touch with what lies 'out there.'"[2] Subtly connected to reality even while detached from it, metaphors retain a great deal of flexibility. When a metaphor appears in

Figure 18.   Blind woman in her hut, with a *dohoné* vessel, Walaqa, Ethiopia,
1984. Photograph by Doron Bacher, courtesy of Beth Hatefutsoth Photo
Archive.

a proverb, it radiates an air of authority which derives from its supposed
antiquity as "the truest remains of the ancient philosophy," one that is
"thus full of hidden meaning."[3]

Numerous studies in recent decades have explored the multiplicity of
meanings to be found in proverbs.[4] All these studies see the proverb as
a formula flexible enough to convey a variety of meanings. It is this quality which makes the proverb such a powerful form of expression, useful
in both understanding and reacting to a complex reality. Without diminishing the importance of context for the study of proverbs, the interviewees themselves were cognizant of the variety of interpretive possibilities that go quite beyond their immediate context. The generation
of meaning within proverbs provides an alternative to the view that meaning is generated primarily by context.[5] By emphasizing the multiplicity
of meanings latent in each proverb and speakers' own awareness of their

exegetic power, these interpretations demonstrate how the metaphorical relationships provide a focal point for a very complex interpretation of reality.

None of this, however, necessarily undermines the substantive value of the metaphors. The very multiplicity may, in fact, even enhance their authenticity as representations of reality. The existence of different but compatible explanations for the same metaphor—rather than different metaphors for different situations—provides group members with a representation of society, while at the same time demonstrating the metaphor's generativity.[6] The different interpretations constitute a kind of perceptual "pool" through which people organize reality—even if only memorized and retrospective—and channel it into basic categories of meaning. These explanations to the proverbs and their metaphors all touch on the relations between Beta Israel and the Christians. Even though the proverbs explicitly reflect different aspects of the daily praxis, the Beta Israel explanations refer to their cosmological meaning.

THE LANGUAGE OF METAPHOR

Because it contains straw, the *dohoné* cannot be fired but must be simply sun-dried, rendering it suitable only for storing dry ingredients such as wheat or barley. The *dohoné* was the only clay vessel made by Christians, and the Beta Israel stressed the fact that no skill was required in making it. In those regions where both religious groups dwelled together, fired vessels were made exclusively by Beta Israel. Thus, calling a Christian a *dohoné* suggested that he was made of inferior, less sophisticated stuff, indeed.

Throughout the interviews, the term *dohoné* stood out as a "key metaphor."[7] It was employed in a number of variations through the course of many interviews and was accompanied by a very broad range of interpretations. The *dohoné* is an example of a metaphor based on self-empowerment whose meaning is axiomatic and self-evident in the minds of the listeners.[8] The *dohoné* was immediately taken for granted as a metaphor for the Christians, which served to render the proverb all the more credible.

Two additional metaphors appear alongside this single key metaphor. The first concerns water and the second fire, and both refer to the Jews. In Ethiopia the Jews were known for dwelling close by sources of running water, the better to fulfill their religious duties of immersion and purification. So frequent were these ritual ablutions that one of the names given the Beta Israel by their non-Jewish neighbours was connected with the scent of water pervading them.[9]

A self-serving metaphor used by Beta Israel was fire. As befits expert potters and blacksmiths, the Beta Israel were known for the smoke that hung over their dwellings.[10] This imagery was reinforced by the Jews with a verse from the Old Testament: "The House of Jacob shall be a fire, and the House of Joseph a flame, and the House of Esau shall be straw; they shall burn it and devour it and no survivor shall be left of the House of Esau, for the Lord has spoken" (Obadiah 1:18).

Inasmuch as Esau was implicitly accepted by the Beta Israel as a metonym for all non-Jews, and especially the Christians, this verse strengthened the metaphorical association and gave it a legitimacy above and beyond that of daily praxis.

As is always the case with metaphorical resonance, the relations of *dohoné,* water, and fire are open to a wide number of interpretations. The group "chose" those interpretations which explained intergroup relations via their own semantic map and which established a number of basic categories for the analysis of a complex and frustrating reality. Let us listen to the interpretations of the informants themselves.

THREE AXIAL PROVERBS

1. The Christian heart is like a *dohoné;*
   wash it, and it falls apart.

This proverb evoked explanations from two basic domains of life. The first comes from the level of daily, personal relations between the two groups and might be paraphrased thus: no matter how much a Jew invests in his relations with a Christian, the relationship is bound to disintegrate. Inevitably, the Christian will betray the Jew. The informants generally illustrated this interpretation by describing areas of common cooperation, such as tenancy arrangements, agricultural labor, and craftsman–client relations. Here the proverb is a warning against Christian unreliability.

The second group of explanations comes from the domain of religion. Christian society traditionally expended considerable effort in the attempt to convert the Beta Israel.[11] While a significant number of them did convert, the informants commonly claimed that they only did so "for appearance's sake." Converted though they were, their hearts were seen as remaining true to Judaism. Indeed, it was the Christians who were seen

as being faithless and inconstant. Such is the tenor of this explanation:
"The Christians' faith, like the *dohoné*, is not strong. See how they make
their *mesqel* [crucifix] themselves. They buy them[12] and then pray to
them; they make all kinds of statues and then pray to them. We pray to
God alone—the faith in our hearts is strong."

The assumption underlying this interpretation is that Christianity lacks
the inner strength of Judaism. The connection between interpretation and
proverb is not immediately comprehensible unless placed in the context
of the Ethiopian reality. In Ethiopia, initiation into both Christianity and
Judaism required immersion in water. Infants of both religions were im-
mersed, as were adults who desired to convert. Immersion was thus one
of the central rites of religious initiation, marking the passage from one
religion to another. The explanation of the proverb demonstrates how
the Beta Israel coped with the fact that conversion was almost exclusively in the direction of Christianity. In reality, a large number of Jews
became Christians, but few Christians became Jews. The proverb tagged
the Christian heart as inconstant and treacherous. Though a member of
Beta Israel might convert, his co-religionists viewed him as having remained "Jewish at heart." In other words, the convert remained unaf-
fected by the water, unlike the *dohoné*, which disintegrated as soon as
it was wet.

Another interesting variation on the theme of religious differences ex-
tends the metaphor of *dohoné* from the Christians themselves to their
doctrines: "Our teachings are good and strong and will hold pure, cold
water. Everyone—Christians and Muslims—have drunk from our teachings, but from their own they cannot. All they have done is to take sections [of our teachings] from various places and write them down in their
book."

This interpretation brings the Old and New Testaments into confrontation. While the *dohoné* was of no use as a drinking vessel, fired
vessels were useful not only for drinking but also for cooling water and
improving its taste. Since Beta Israel provided all the drinking vessels in
regions where they lived, this praxis formed the basis for the idea by which
all religions benefited from Judaism as from a draught of cold water. But
Christianity, as a *dohoné*, could not fulfill any such task and hence could
not be "imbibed."

A variation of this idea claims that the Christian religion is "half-
baked":[13] "Just as water destroys the *dohoné*, so the *Orit* destroys their
faith." By likening the Old Testament to fire, which the *dohoné* must
avoid, it follows that Christians must also beware of the Old Testament

lest they—unlike the fired Jewish vessels—be burned and consumed. There is yet another variation of this theme: "We call our teachings *berhan,* light; our teachings are the fire. The Christians are like the *dohoné,* without fire: their teachings are not strong like ours."

Finally, it should be noted that some informants, when describing the *dohoné* vessel and the way it dissolved in water, quoted the Biblical verse, "from dust it comes and to dust it will return" (Genesis 3:19). Indeed, as will be seen further on, this point would seem to be most significant in understanding the manner in which the Beta Israel perceived the *dohoné* imagery and, by extension, the relations between the two groups.

II. **The Christian heart resembles a *dohoné;*
no matter how much you clean it, dirty it remains.**

In this proverb, cleaning the vessel is a frustrating task: the cleaning process succeeds only in adding a new layer of mud to the unfired clay vessel, making it all the dirtier. Informants explained the reality behind this proverb in two ways. First, just as there is never a time when the *dohoné* is not dirty, neither can the Christians ever be clean, inasmuch as their religion is based on the sin of idol worship, that is, praying to the crucifix and to icons. Second, there is no point in trying to convince a Christian that we are not *kayla* or *buda* [maleficent spirits] and that we do not open graves in search of corpses. He might seem, for a moment, to understand, but then, if something happens to him or his family, he will blame you again. So, just as the dirt cannot be removed from the *dohoné,* neither can the superstitions be removed from the Christians.

III. ***Dohoné:* from water it was made
and water it will hate.**

Without water, the *dohoné* could not have been made. Yet, once created, it cannot bear the touch of water. The paradox of destruction by the creator is widely known in cultures cognate to Beta Israel, as well as in those located further afield.[14] In the present context, however, the focus centers on the paradox of the proverb and its metaphorical relation to the social reality of the Ethiopian Jewish minority. Like the two examples cited above, this proverb was also interpreted by the Beta Israel in terms of relations between the two groups in Ethiopian society.[15] While the last word in this proverb has been translated as hate, it also has connotations of fear and was interpreted by some informants in both senses, as the following examples will show:

A. Hatred

My partners in dialogue mentioned that "although [Christianity] is derived from Judaism, Christians hate it [Judaism]." Through this they conveyed not only a sense of Christian ingratitude but also a feeling of being utterly scorned and reviled by the Christians. Whereas the speakers explained this proverb in terms of the relationship between the two groups, it may ultimately reflect the ongoing religious polemic in which the two religions are seen in terms of a father and child relationship, with all the indignation and pain that filial ingratitude can bring.[16]

B. Fear

Three basic explanations involved fear:

1. "The Christians are afraid of us. The Jews know how to make everything—we make them their plows, their tools, their cooking pots, and even their weapons. We have the power to make all these and so they are afraid of us—they are afraid that one day we will become stronger and rule over them."

2. "The *dohoné* is made of straw and so cannot be fired. If it were put in the fire it would fall to pieces."

3. "Despite the fact that Christianity is descended from Judaism, the Christians are afraid to dispute with us. Whenever we argued religion with them, they ran away. They don't want to know the truth—they are afraid of the truth, the Old Testament."

The power of water or fire to destroy the *dohoné* reflects a basic Beta Israel concept. The Jews were regarded as being more powerful than their neighbors, both in their own eyes and in the eyes of the Christians. Interviewers also expressed the idea that the inferior status of the Jews in Ethiopia was the result of God's will, a test to which He was subjecting them. Just as they had once ruled a significant part of Ethiopia, so in the future would their rule again be restored.

On another level, this proverb may be interpreted differently. While admittedly not used by the Beta Israel, it would seem to be consistent with their semantic field. In the frequent religious debates so well known to the Beta Israel, the Christians held their Jewish neighbors responsible for the crucifixion of Jesus. This accusation, unconsciously internalized by the Jews, might lead to the following explanation: just as the water which creates the *dohoné* ultimately destroys it, so the creator of Christianity was ultimately undone by his own people.

PROVERB AS CORRECTIVE:
THE DEEPER SOCIAL EXEGESIS

The interpretations of these proverbs arrayed the Christian / dohoné metaphor against the two metaphors for the Beta Israel, fire and water. These proverbs captured a confusing and frequently painful reality by funneling daily events into categories of significance.[17] The explanations given the proverbs show how the Beta Israel chose to view their social reality, but that is not all. The manner in which these explanations were molded into categories of significance also facilitates analysis beyond the conscious level of explanation and permits us to learn more about the cultural patterns in which the informants functioned as well as the cultural reservoir from which their explanations were drawn.

The interpretations presented above are strongly metonymic. While water and fire are representative of the Beta Israel they are also, by extension, representative of the Orit itself. In similar fashion, the dohoné metaphor could also be interpreted as referring either to the Christians or to their New Testament teachings. So closely was each group of religionists identified with its beliefs that the discussion could move freely from one to the other without any sense of dissonance or incongruity.

The dohoné was closely connected with water, just as, on a daily level, the Christians and Jews also were joined in a single context. A dohoné could only be made by mixing soil with water. For though its body was composed of soil, its malleability was determined by water—and water could also cause the dohoné to revert to its former shapeless state. Hence the significance of the Biblical passage already noted above, "from dust it comes and to dust it will return" (Genesis 3:19). Just as God breathed life into Adam and made him a human being, so did Judaism, or, at a more metonymic level, the Old Testament, give life to Christianity. Water gave life to dust, creating an entity—the dohoné. Without water it would simply be dust once again. The relationship, then, is a hierarchy of creator and created, one that stresses the ephemeral nature of Christianity and the eternal nature of Judaism. This point also finds expression in the much-emphasized ease with which a dohoné could be made—any woman or child in Ethiopia could do it. Thus the application of the dohoné metaphor also represents an attempt to associate the Christians with an inferior, less sophisticated vessel.

Descriptions of Jewish daily life clearly reveal its inherent complexity and demonstrate a keen awareness of Christian domination. Beta Israel's interpretation of the proverbs, however, betrays a model which acted as a corrective. On the basis of this analysis, a distinction should be drawn between the two levels of interpretation. The first was drawn from the realm of daily praxis, seen for the most part as negative and confusing; the second comes from the realm of cosmology and was used by the Beta Israel as a corrective device for restoring the emotional equilibrium and imposing a certain sense and meaning to the frustrations of daily life. Perhaps in ordinary life the Christians were masters of the Ethiopian soil, but in cosmological terms they were far less exalted—*dohoné*, as it were, a composite of mud and straw. The Beta Israel, on the other hand, were the fire and water created by the word of God during the six days of creation. The *dohoné*, therefore, dwelt at a lower stage of creation or, at least, farther away from God. In this view, the Beta Israel were pure and untainted God-created elements, while the Christians were man-made and hence could not be the result of divine revelation. Moreover, even when considered as a product of human culture, Christianity was incomplete; the *dohoné* existed in a weak, intermediate form. No longer a pure, natural element, such as water or earth, neither had it been transformed into a strong, fired vessel.

By linking themselves with fire, fired vessels, and water, the Beta Israel were in essence connecting themselves to the powerful, basic forces of God's universe. By associating the Christians with the soil through the *dohoné* metaphor, they were leaving them with their land, true enough, but a land which was almost worthless, according to the corrective model, without water and fire to strengthen and mold it. On both the descriptive and metaphorical levels, therefore, the Beta Israel endowed themselves with a legitimacy and even a certain supremacy denied them by the Christians.

Being a flexible formula perceived as "authentic" and bearing the authority of tradition, while at the same time able to accommodate a rich variety of meanings, the proverb holds great interpretive power both for understanding a complex, multifaceted, and changing reality and for responding to it. In the eyes of the people studied, the use of contrasting metaphors to represent the wide variety of perceptions of such complex social relations reinforced the authenticity of those metaphors as accurate representations of reality. The metaphorical relations served, then, as a multidimensional prism for reality interpretation. The Beta Israel used proverb and key metaphors beyond their immediate, discursive context, exegetically, to construct and reconstruct their past, explaining their relations with their Christian neighbors within the retrospective reflexive context of our interviews. The concept of "context" was thereby broadened beyond its usual sense. The researcher became one link in an interpretive chain of multilayered explicative work.[18] The work of interpretation lies not in superimposing explanations on phenomena hitherto uninterpreted but in defining the researcher's place in this interpretive chain and in the flow of insights inspired by the research dialogue.

An examination of the speakers' interpretations of these three metaphors suggests a perceptual system laden with transformations which employs materials, forms, and terms from daily life as metonymies and metaphors for the relations between the two groups and their respective religions. These explanations constitute an exegetical system that manifestly relates to the transformations encapsulated in the proverbs. The explanatory system grants corrective meaning to the inconsistent and contradictory intergroup reality also articulated in other forms.

The metaphorical links between water and fire set off associative links between the metaphors themselves, on the one hand, and between the metaphors and reality, on the other. These associations may be further illuminated in psychoanalytical terms as primary processes of linkage. The identification of Beta Israel with water or fire and of the Christians with the *dohoné* generates a dichotomous, transformative hierarchy of creator and product, cause and effect. Beta Israel present themselves as a source, an inalterable material, while the Christians are depicted as subject to metamorphosis. In the interpretation that accompanies the proverbs under discussion, the transformative process follows two directions— shaping and dismantlement. Both processes are thus perceived, symbolically, as formative processes.

The conceptualization of transformative processes, including the basic religious transformation according to which Christianity is a metamorphosis of Judaism, emerged in other forms of articulation as well. However, this grand transformation, as well as its repercussive transformations, is presented in a clearer and more direct way in proverbs than in other forms of expression.

The dichotomy that hints at the permanent versus the transitory, contained in the metaphorical opposition of water and fire (Jews) and *dohoné* (Christians), reflects a recognition that Christianity is based on a process of transformation.

Being water, the Beta Israel have invincible hearts that do not melt even during baptism, and they remain firm in their faith. In contrast, the Christians, as *dohoné,* are not strong of faith and they believe simultaneously in the power of Judaism.

The system of oppositions familiar to the Beta Israel from their everyday reality were processed and recognized through the proverbial prism. Thus the metaphors, their expression in proverbs, and their interpretation channeled complexity into simple, abstract forms and simultaneously opened new meanings of concretization in vivid detail. The proverb's dependence on vocabulary taken from the field of everyday crafts, their materials, and the ways they are processed, directed the gaze to the primal foundations of existence. The familiar contradictions of daily life were thus imposed on primal cosmological principles.

Proverbial-metaphorical articulation produces, more than any other form of articulation present in our interviews, a *corrective meaning,* different and even opposite to other forms. This corrective meaning relates to variations of opposing categories in the life of the group, whose existence the Beta Israel saw as contradictory and confusing. The system of opposing categories also relates to the broader system of opposites in the life of the group in a corrective, remedial way.

As fire and water, the Beta Israel identified themselves with the *active forces of nature* and thus also as close to God Himself. In contrast, Christianity and the Christians were presented as *dohoné,* as earth, whose capacity to bring forth life depends on the presence of active transforming power. This opposition had a parallel on the daily level of praxis, inasmuch as the Beta Israel tenants worked the land of the Christians. The transformation on the proverb level took on an independent and coherent configuration presented in poetic language. As such, it constituted a transformation with a special status, the uniqueness of which lay in its relative isolation from direct social contexts. The proverbs, invoked retrospectively, assumed a corrective quality on an abstract level that was not possible to the same extent in other forms of articulation, which were subject to direct social interaction.

CHAPTER 12

Transformations

This work is the chronicle of an attempt to capture a consciousness of a reality that is foreign to the most fundamental categories of modern Western thought. One of the most basic of these is the theorem of the constancy of real objects. As an unspoken assumption, the theorem asserts that objects and people do not spontaneously transform themselves from what they are into something else.[1] For example, the notion that a person could be an ordinary man by day and a hyena by night is something the Western mind could grasp only as a nightmarish fantasy.

Even though I had been educated as an anthropologist, trained to accept the exotic, the sheer fact that people sitting across from me, speaking Hebrew in an Israeli apartment, were relating this to me casually, as a matter of course, shocked me. My own need for constancy and coherence continually impelled me to seek them where there was little or none.

There was a risk that my attempt to satisfy a need for logical consistency would compromise the speakers' inner acceptance of the natural incoherence of things. I was coming from a context that set up a dichotomous separation between Jews and non-Jews. It assumed there could be a clear-cut answer to the question, "Are the Falasha real Jews?" whereas I was asking, "What did it mean to be a Jew in Ethiopia?" After months of a failing search for a principle which would accommodate the apparent contradictions and inconsistencies of what I was hearing, I had to rethink the traditional formulation of the question itself. Another answer was staring at me out of the chaos of the materials themselves. The emerging Ethiopian reality was simply this: reality is constantly transforming, renewing, and contradicting itself—and challenging us.

In a culture which accepted as natural the transformation of things and beings into their opposites, would it not seem to follow that Judaism and Christianity, Jews and Christians, were mutually transformable? Even raising the question of such a possibility was the gravest Jewish heresy. Even so, the possibility for the "same" and its opposite to exist simultaneously lay at the root of much of the wonder, understanding, certainty, and doubt which fused together to form the Ethiopian consciousness within Beta Israel.

As we proceeded, a schema of Jewish–Christian relations emerged that combined a model centered on religious separation (emphasizing segmentation) with a model of connectedness (emphasizing continuity). Transformation linked the two models, with each in turn taken up, or put aside, in the different areas of contact between the two groups. This combination derived originally from the most basic transformative connection—the one between the two religions—which was of immense importance to Beta Israel, who repeated and reformulated it at all levels of their existence.

This concluding chapter, then, will be devoted to a discussion of the most important issue in the accumulation of actions and beliefs which connect—in form and content—all the various means of cultural expression. The belief in the transformation of people, material, and forms characterized intergroup relations in Ethiopia, occurring in different areas and at various levels of manifestation and always assuming different forms.[2] Transformation was ubiquitous in all aspects of this study and emerged as the central idiom in Jewish–Christian relations in Ethiopia.

As the study progressed, the salience of the transformative became clear. Scientific discourse had to reflect the governing ethnographic syntax. Members of the group emphasized the transformative passages between the categories, and their energy and animation increased when concentrated upon examining these transmutations.

Examples are legion. Beta Israel were not distinguished from their Christian neighbors by any physical, visual, or linguistic differences and would seem to have belonged to a single group. However, it was precisely on the physical level that contact between Jews and Christians was forbidden, on the grounds that it led to contamination and transferred impurity. The Christians, for their part, also refrained from close contact with Beta Israel, out of fear of magical curses. Both groups developed different mechanisms designed to enable routine daily ties between them. The descriptions of the techniques used to circumvent the transference of impurity included "antidotes," such as wet green branches, animal feces, and water, used for purification by immersion. These materials are all unstable, in the sense that they belong simultaneously to two contradictory categories: animate / inanimate, wet / dry, and even alive / dead. It is possible that the very instability of these materials enabled the logical connection between them and their ability to cancel the transference of impurity. Thus, for instance, water, as a transformative element, appeared in other forms and even on more abstract levels of expression, such as religious conversion (ritual immersion) and, metaphorically, in proverbs.

Economic ties between the two groups were based on a hierarchical structure in which firm cooperation existed in the areas of agriculture and livestock tending as well as the crafts in which Jews specialized. In order to explain to me the nature of the work relations between the groups, my informants resorted to a language replete with contrasts and transformations. The land, the main source of livelihood for Jews and Christians alike, belonged to the Christians, and Beta Israel worked it as tenants. The inequality and unfairness of this situation was apparent also in explanations of the appellations Christians gave to Jews. The Jews' belief in their ancient roots in Ethiopia was incompatible with the Christian denial of their right to own land. The claims raised by the Christians to justify their ownership of the land indicated to the Jews an awareness that the Jews once owned extensive lands and potentially might do so again.

The specialized crafts practiced by Beta Israel were highly charged with transformative tensions. The men worked as smiths and the women made pottery, two crafts engaged in the mutation of materials and forms, especially through the use of fire. The Christians had a highly ambivalent attitude toward these occupations: the crafts and the craftsmen were considered inferior, but the products were in great demand. In an agricultural society dependent on clay utensils, work implements, knives, and weapons, Beta Israel and their products represented the dependence of the strong upon the inferior and weak. More significantly, the products created by Beta Israel were used for the basic transformations of agriculture, animal slaughter, and cooking. Jews presented these implements to Christians as presents at ritual occasions, emphasizing the symbolic content of the cooperation between the groups and the role Beta Israel occupied in the social structure in Ethiopia. Their crafts were also believed to be endowed with a power linked to the transmogrification of souls from human to superhuman (and extra-human). The ambivalence with which these crafts were regarded was expressed by the attribution of supernatural powers to the craftsmen. Their supernatural powers endowed their products with a special quality. The sinister aura attached to these crafts was also associated with the image of the hyena (*buda*). The Jews were believed to have originally had the form of a hyena, incarnated in daily life into a human being. This belief was linked to the consumption of food in Ethiopian culture: it was believed that the *buda*, in order to survive, would dig up newly buried corpses, particularly those of babies, and suck their blood.

Nevertheless, the *ritual domain*, like the economic one, also afforded many opportunities for positive relations; members of each group participated in religious holidays and family affairs of the other group (especially weddings and funerals). I was told that Christians who participate in the Sigd listened to prayers in Ge'ez and "took joy in the Torah," while Beta Israel regarded Christian celebrations from afar. Likewise, Christians would ask Beta Israel to pray for them during the holidays and even to offer sacrifices. This type of request was not reciprocated by the Jews.

The holidays of Beta Israel provided an especially apt opportunity for the Christians to invoke the divine power. Beta Israel, representing the Old Testament and Judaism, were believed to possess special powers and a unique closeness to the shared divinity. When a Christian would request an intervention that was fulfilled, he would offer donations and gifts to the books of the *Orit*, the Jewish priests, and the house of prayer.

The mutual regard expressed by each group for the other's *religious holidays* illustrates the complexity of the relations between the groups. In Jewish descriptions of Christian holidays and practices, all familiar to them, it was clear that great attraction and interest coexisted with discomfort and scorn. The scorn often surfaced in descriptions of the icons used by the Christians. "The image of Miriam" (Mary) was set against the Torah (*Orit*). This opposition was also stressed in relation to the Temqat celebration (baptism), the archetype of a fundamental transformation in Christianity: namely, the Jewish Jesus becoming a Christian. Similar details in the descriptions of the way the Christians celebrated this holiday emphasized the differences between the two groups: Beta Israel prayed by holding a Torah codex wrapped in fabric, while the Christians held wooden icons, also wrapped in fabric. The Judaism / Christianity transition was presented as a passage from the belief in a holy book to belief in an idol, or from belief in "truth" to belief in "falsehood." These sets of binary oppositions—truth / falsehood, book / icon—derived from a more fundamental split in which one religion was a transmutation of the other. The dialogue between the two groups probed the significance of this transformation and the issue of primacy based on it.

The baptism festival, Temqat, was the Christian holiday that elicited the greatest response in the interviews, being an annual reminder of the baptism of Jesus, the Jew, to Christianity. The accounts we heard were marked by great ambivalence: the festivities themselves were described as fascinating and attractive, but the specific practices revealed the falsehood of Christianity itself. This ambivalence toward the fundamental historical-religious progression from Judaism to Christianity was reenacted over and over on the level of daily reality, with members of Beta Israel "progressing" to Christianity by undergoing baptism.

Converts were prominently exposed to the tense dialectic between ethnicity and religion. When the religious boundary—the most fundamental border between the groups—was breached, the ethnic element gained strength as the cutting edge of the intergroup differences. The distinction between the groups was then reformulated as a passage from a religious to an ethnic group. In the relations between Jews and Christians, blood figured as the basic symbol linking God with His believers. It was the primary emblem of group identification, and lay at the heart of the religious rivalry between the two groups. Anything related to blood raised strong emotions. Disputes over menstruation, ritual slaughter, and the eating of blood were not open to negotiation. Sheerly as a spectacle, any outpouring of blood is startling, if not ominous. When the physical spectacle is further loaded with religious significance, its fatefulness is accentuated. Blood not only sustains the body; it gives sustenance to the soul, and it seals and sanctifies one's religious identity. Like a river flowing between two nations, it forms a clear and hopefully defensible boundary.

But the frequency of actual conversions demonstrated how easily this border could be transgressed. The resulting conflict between inviolability and violation made it all the more urgent to defend in principle what was flouted in practice.

These transformations found expression in the realm of proverbs and metaphors. Beta Israel, as fire and water, perceived themselves as the creative forces of nature, and for this reason were closer to God. Christianity and Christians were *dohoné,* earth, whose fertility requires the generative action of sun and rain. This symbolic opposition found a parallel in the daily praxis: Beta Israel as the serfs working land owned by Christians. The transformation on the level of proverbs was expressed in an independent, coherent expressive system, in poetic language. As such it was a transformation enjoying special status, unique in its relative isolation from direct social contexts. The dichotomy of eternity versus temporality contained in the metaphorical opposition of water and fire (Jews) to *dohoné* (Christians) reflected the belief (on the symbolic level) in their own greater ability to withstand the transformations threatened by change, compared with Christianity—itself a product of religious transformation.

The story of my encounter with the Beta Israel through a highly detailed, dialogic ethnography emerged as a confrontation on a much more fundamental level between two different and basically opposed models of thinking: the Western idea of the constancy of objects and the Ethiopian transformative model. As this confrontation came to a head in my own work, it created an opening for understanding that this meeting of conceptual worlds also shaped the contemporary physical and political encounter between Beta Israel and world Jewry. Since Judaism today is anchored in Western conceptions, the question concerning Beta Israel's identity could not have been fashioned in any frame of reference other than through binary coordinates, reflected in the definitive question, "Are the Falasha *real* Jews?"

The fascination of Jews worldwide with the Beta Israel was more than mere appeal to an "exotic" isolated Jewish group in the heart of Africa. It resonated from far greater depths. The discovery of co-religionists perceived as racially "other" sparked fundamental questions of Jewish identity and aroused latent tensions between race and religion in Judaism.[3] The discourse regarding the identity of the Ethiopian Jews, which took place across the entire Jewish world, therefore focused on origins, raising various speculations regarding the Beta Israel's presence in Ethiopia.

It was therefore not surprising that the Sephardic Chief Rabbi of Israel, based on a rabbinic decision from four centuries earlier, issued a ruling that the group was descended from the lost tribe of Dan. This ruling, based on the myth of shared Jewish origins, illuminates the paradox inherent when sensitivity over eugenic distinctions based on "race" mingle with the primacy of descent in Jewish identity. Significantly, the rabbinic proclamation linked the Beta Israel to the Jewish people in a way that did not challenge the underlying presumption of Jewish common descent.

The very assumption that the question of Jewish authenticity should serve as the focus of the discourse on Beta Israel identity implies a non-transformative Judaism bound by uniform criteria and fixed boundaries. From a normative Jewish viewpoint, these fixed boundaries are fundamental to Judaism and a source of religious pride.

For the Beta Israel, who were for a long period cut off from other Jewish communities, the question of Jewish identity was governed by the organizing dynamic of transformation and was, as this book demonstrates, profoundly related to Christianity. The drama of their position as a marginal group in Christian Ethiopia, however, was transformed to an internal Jewish drama when they encountered the Jewish world outside Ethiopia. The conceptual confrontation between the fixed boundaries of normative Judaism and the fluid Ethiopian model was central to this drama and assumed expression in the metaphor of skin color.

Upon their arrival in Israel, the Ethiopian immigrants, with their undeniably different external appearance, were immediately seen as anomalous to the absorbing society. While in Ethiopia they had regarded themselves as being light-skinned in relation to the *barya* ("red" vs. "black"), in Israel another color scale was at work. A terminology of black and white came into play and the Ethiopians found themselves being termed simply "black," without any distinction of shade. Internalizing these normative Jewish perceptions, there were those who sought to assure themselves that, being Jews, they were not intrinsically black. This belief was supported by a quaint article of faith, that many generations of exposure to the African sun had burnished their original whiteness. "When we arrive in Israel," they told one another, "our dark color will fade away and the real Jews among us will finally be seen for what we really are: white."

Here, as with religion, a transformation was expected. But the magic never happened, and the static, Western model of constancy held reign. Confronted with the embarrassing fact that in this case transformation did not occur, the Beta Israel fell back on a variety of rationalizations. Some said that the change would take longer. Some claimed to have seen the coming of the change in the relatively lighter skin of their newborn in Israel. Others accepted their unchanged color as proof that Judaism was more than skin deep.

I began this work with a general query: "What does it mean to be a Jew in Christian Ethiopia?" When Jewish religious authorities were debating the issue of admitting the Falashas to Israel, the question they had to answer was, "Are the Falasha real Jews?" But from the outset this was never a purely religious question, and in one guise—or disguise—or another, identity problems persist, providing a challenging opportunity for reformulating the overall query. The question should not be "Are the Falasha real Jews?" but rather, "What does it mean to be a Jew in the first place?"

The ethnography of Jewish life in Christian Ethiopia, and particularly the cultural manifestations and organizing principles governing Beta Israel's experience, allow for a more inclusive conception of Judaism as a cultural system. The racial "otherness" and "deviant" Judaism of Beta Israel challenge simplistic assumptions about the physical and spiritual unity of the Jewish people and are a catalyst for the exploration of Judaism in a much wider cultural framework. Their very identity presents an opportunity to reconceive Judaism not through the imposition of external considerations of common origin or even religious practice but through an internal frame of reference. As Jewish identity is refracted through the prism of Beta Israel's experience, Judaism will continue to reveal itself in a dynamic and not always coherent fashion, joining competing voices and engaged in multiple and changing dialogues.

Notes

INTRODUCTION

1. *Qes* is the term used for both Christian and Jewish priests in Ethiopia.

2. Although usually referred to as Falasha, they themselves use the name "Beta Israel" (the House of Israel) to refer to their life in Ethiopia.

3. The exodus began in 1977 and continued with Operation Moses in 1984 and Operation Solomon in 1991. These were preceded by the momentous halakhic decision of Israel's Chief Sephardic Rabbi, Ovadiah Yosef. In 1973, basing his opinion on rabbinic tradition from 400 years earlier, he ruled that the Falashas—as the descendants of the lost tribe of Dan—were Jews. See also Kaplan and Rosen (1993: 35), Rapoport (1981), and the recent study on their modern history by Summerfield (1997). On the halakhic status of Ethiopian Jews, see Chelouche (1988), Corinaldi (1988), and Waldman (1989, 1991).

4. For a discussion of the ethnography of memory, see, for example, Bahloul (1996), Boyarin (1991), and Fischer (1986).

5. For other historical studies and speculations, see note 8 below.

6. They also have other books, but it became clear during the interviews that the *Orit* was most central to their self-identity as a group. On other books sacred to them, see Kaplan (1989) and Shelemay (1989). Ge'ez is the language of the Holy Books—Christian and Jewish alike—in Ethiopia.

7. Among the early writers who treated the group as a clearly defined entity, the following traveler-scholars are prominent: Bruce (1805), Faitlovitch (1905), and Halévy (1877, 1906). The latter two, European Jews, were sent to Ethiopia in quest of traces of the "lost tribe," whose existence as a remote Jewish group sparked the imagination and emotions of many, especially Jews, in the West. These travelers were instrumental in endowing Ethiopian Jews with their image as the "lost tribe." Their publications emphasized points of similarity between Beta Israel and Jews elsewhere in the world and portrayed them as an isolated Jewish

diaspora living for long years as pariahs among hostile foreign surroundings. Protestant ministers who were sent to convert them to Christianity also emphasized the difference and uniqueness of their religion and customs compared to those of the Christian in Ethiopia, though their motivation in stressing the uniqueness was totally different. See Flad (1869), Gobat (1850), and Stern (1968). This emphasis continued to figure prominently in the studies by researchers who came later (Aeŝcoly [1943], Kessler [1982], Messing [1982], and Wurmbrand [1971], and to a large degree the studies of Hess [1969]). Despite the different sources they drew upon for their studies, they all resorted to historical speculation regarding origins. They emphasized Ethiopian Jewry's social and religious uniqueness and presented the Jewish presence in Ethiopia as a product of intercommunal struggle. This presentation made Beta Israel appear almost totally self-determined and isolated from their surroundings. To this stream may be added studies that implicitly strengthened this model by dealing with intergroup aspects and tended to ignore the existence of the group within the wider Ethiopian context (Ben Dor [1985a, 1987], Schoenberger [1975]). For an annotated bibliography on the Beta Israel, see Kaplan and Ben Dor (1988) and Salamon and Kaplan (1998).

8. As contrasted to the "lost tribe" model, the "integrated group" model views the Beta Israel community as an integral part of wider Ethiopian history and culture. It emphasizes the many similarities between Beta Israel and their Christian neighbors and cites their inclusion in the wider social setting. This is especially true for the historical studies by Kaplan (1992a), Quirin (1977, 1992), and Shelemay (1989), who suggested that Beta Israel emerged from a schism between Christian sects in the fifteenth century. This integral model has gained strength in scholarly circles (Conti Rossini [1928], Krempel [1972, 1974], Ullendorff [1968, 1973], and to a certain degree Leslau [1951]). It is typical of this trend that even scholars who do not confine themselves to the historical conclusions reached by Kaplan, Quirin, and Shelemay could no longer ignore, as in the past, the wider Ethiopian context and its centrality to the study of Beta Israel. Presenting the group as one group within the conglomerate of religious collectivities in Ethiopia is also typical of literature pertaining to culture and society in general. See especially Cerulli (1956), Conti Rossini (1937), Pollers (1940), Rathjens (1921), Simoons (1960), Abbink (1984, 1987, 1990), Levine (1974), Lipsky (1962), and Shack (1974).

9. The dialogue with Christian communities has recently become one of the main avenues in studying Jewish history, e.g., Yuval (forthcoming), Boyarin (1998, 1999), and Hasan-Rokem (1996, especially ch. 8).

10. Such as the Qemant. On this group, see Gamst (1969) and Kaplan (1992a: 160).

11. This tension was magnified because I sought a fuller understanding of the Ethiopia that exists inside them. The mechanisms of memory selection constitute both a challenge and an obstacle for the researcher. For a study of the architecture of memory in a North African Jewish community, see Bahloul (1996).

12. Geertz (1988:1).

13. The exception to this was in the Wolqait region, as I shall elaborate in the coming chapters.

CHAPTER 1.   INSULTS AND CIPHERS

1. See the map of regions and villages inhabited by Jews (fig. 5).

2. See Abbink (1990).

3. On the various names and physical structure of the prayer house and the "houses of blood," see also Schoenberger (1975). On these "bloody" separation periods, see "Menstruation," in chapter 10 of this book.

4. For a more detailed discussion, see Aešcoly (1943), Leslau (1951), and Schoenberger (1975). On the laws of purity and impurity, contact and avoidance, that are also known as the Attenkugn laws, and their historical development, see Kaplan (1992a: 132, 134–135). Historical testimonies from relatively late periods emphasize Beta Israel's strict adherence to the prohibition against physical contact with anyone who was not a part of their group. On this issue, see Aešcoly (1943: 217, 219, 278), Gobat (1850: 10), and Halévy (1877).

5. Green branches were viewed as a material which does not transmit impurity. They were used in various contexts to separate the impure from the pure. This theme will be further discussed.

6. These clay cups, which were manufactured by the Jewish women, were cheaper than other cups made of bull or cow horns and could be considered disposable.

7. Gamst (1969), Kaplan (1988, 1992a), and Taddesse (1988).

8. See, for example, Simoons (1960: 35).

9. Buxton (1970: 44–46), Sergew (1972), and Taddesse (1988: 241). The extent to which legitimacy of government is tied genealogically to the tribes of Israel can be seen in the attempt made on the part of the Zagwa tribe to link itself (by means of two myths) to the Israelite genealogy. While the Ethiopian church views the Zagwe tribe as an illegitimate dynasty, because its rulers are not descendants of the tribes of Israel, the historical leaders coming from this tribe claimed a double bond to Moses and his "Cushite" wife Zipporah (Numbers 12:1) and to King Solomon—through a handmaiden of the Queen of Sheba. See Sergew (1972: 241). The second mythological version was mentioned in the interviews

10. This conflict is epitomized in the Christians' view (as described by the Jews) of the reign of Queen Yudit, called Gudith—"the bad"—by them, and is described as "the strong queen of the Falasha" (Budge [1928: 153–154] and Kaplan [1992a: 44–47]), and one of the greatest enemies of Christianity and the Solomonistic dynasty in Ethiopia. It appears that the Christians perceived this power as a dangerous potential which should remain oppressed. An interesting comparison can be made to another cultural context: a well-known North African legend describes a Jewish woman saint-leader (A-Cahina) whose political power and potential are fixed in the consciousness of local Muslims (Goldberg [1992]). The Jewish woman leader in Ethiopia may symbolize, in a similar fashion, the potential for power castration of the dominant group at the hands of the minority.

11. Particularly in the Belesa, Lasta, Wogera, and Gondar regions.

12. There were very close ties between the Tigre and the Wolqait regions. See Salamon (1986).

13. See, for example, Kaplan (1992a: 65ff.). For possible historical and se-

mantic sources for this term in Ethiopia, see Rosen (1985a: 54–56). See also Weil's (1995) overview of "collective designations" among Ethiopian Jews.

14. Two additional explanations were suggested in the interviews: The Tigrinya verb *felisu* means "removed from his land"—willfully or otherwise. According to the interviewees, the Ge'ez term *felasa* means "went," "went off," and even "went and converted." The discussion is not linguistic but sociological, and thus it is the explanations offered by the informants that are of importance. This last explanation may serve to strengthen the claim of a number of prominent historians that the Jews were originally Christians who broke off from mainstream Christianity over issues of doctrinal and ritual practice in the fifteenth century and over the years developed an identity of Jewishness (See Kaplan [1992a], Quirin [1977, 1992], and Shelemay [1989]). On the other hand, many speakers attributed a different meaning to the term *falasha*, claiming that it contains the fear of them as possessors of supernatural powers. I suggest understanding this as a double connection: the most characteristic image of Beta Israel—possessors of magical powers—radiated onto the appellation "Falasha," and this, in turn, was interpreted as an accusation. Yet it appears that this very central conception, that being foreign and unlanded has to do with power in general and with supernatural powers in particular, is central in this interpretation of the term. The power of this conception was attested to in many interviews and in a variety of contexts. Thus, for instance, in the aforementioned suggestion, many informants said that it was common to say of them that they—like other unlanded groups—"aren't afraid," "don't have anything to lose," and can easily move from one region to another. Disputes between landed people must be resolved immediately in order to reestablish equilibrium, while Jewish–Christian disputes must be resolved in compromise. It is easier for the Jew to cause damage and then flee the region. It seems that this assessment was grounded in reality. Throughout the interviews there were reports of Jews who wanted to take vengeance on those who had leveled accusations of magical behavior against them (to the point of physical injury to the accuser). These were accompanied by comments as to their lack of attachment to their home region and the possibility of finding shelter in distant villages which had Jewish inhabitants. It is no coincidence that the appellation "Falasha" was less common in Tigre and Wolqait, the only regions in which Jews had ownership (be it partial or full) of land and family continuity in a fixed area. Correspondingly, fewer magical accusations were made against the Jews in these areas.

15. Quirin does not explain the meaning of the term but says only that it is in Agaw (the language) and came into currency in the seventeenth century (1992, note 2). D'Abbadie (1851–1852) claims that Abba Itzhak, one of the Falasha leaders, explained the term as meaning "those who would not cross [the river]," according to the tradition identifying Beta Israel as descendants of the Israelites who accompanied Manelik I and refused to cross the river on Sabbath. On this point see Kaplan (1990a: 153) and Rosen (1985a).

16. Another documented name, also connected to the Jew's strict observance of purity and impurity rules, is the term "Attenkugn." Meaning "touch-me-not," it refers both to Beta Israel's strict laws of ritual purity and, through their reluctance to have any physical contact with a non-Jew, to the group itself.

17. See also Kaplan (1992a: 195–196, note 23) and Rosen (1985a:56–57).

18. It is not the linguistic aspect of this connection which is here examined, but the socio-cultural. This explanation is typical of a wide phenomenon, which lies outside the purview of the current study: immigrants from various regions in Ethiopia suggested explanations which trace the names of locations in Ethiopia to Hebrew. According to them, it is only after arriving in Israel and learning Hebrew that they could understand the original meaning of names of geographic locations in Ethiopia. It appears, then, that even in Israel they remain concerned with Israelite roots in Ethiopia, in an attempt to provide additional legitimization of their historic link to Israel.

19. For studies examining and comparing their physical traits, see Sheba et al. (1962) and Zoosmann-Diskin (1991).

20. For a more detailed discussion of the region and the languages spoken in it, see Salamon (1986: 12–17).

21. On Beta Israel's intra-group signals, see also Salamon (1987). For a similar discussion regarding the Jews of southern Iran, see Loeb (1977). On "secret languages" as characteristic of intergroup boundaries, see Lamar-Ross (1978: 6–8).

22. For a description of similar in-group vocabulary among Jews in southern Iran, see Loeb (1977).

23. Salamon (1986).

CHAPTER 2.   CHRISTIAN LAND, SABBATH MILK, AND THE MAGIC OF FIRE

1. Officially, the Ethiopian Communist revolution of 1974 brought an end to the leasing of private lands, but the interviewees were adamant in their claims that they did not benefit from land redistribution. On the systems of land tenure in Ethiopia, see Crummey (1980), Donham and James (1986), and Hoben (1970, 1973).

2. Hoben (1970), in writing about patron–client relations among Amharic Christians, claims that the patron–client relationship entails advantages to both sides: the patron provides security, defense, and material benefits, while the client supports his patron and is faithful to him. The descriptions of the informants provide, however, only limited support for Hoben's analysis, as the relations between Beta Israel and the Christians were based on the group aspect of the two communities.

3. See also Crummey (1980: 130).

4. In this regard it is interesting to compare Jewish–Muslim relations in Morocco (Rosen [1972: 160]). On this notion, see Scott (1985) and Turner (1969).

5. My fieldwork revealed a great deal of evidence regarding Beta Israel's mobility. See also Salamon (1986).

6. A number of historical studies (Kaplan [1992a], Quirin [1977, 1992]) point to the connection between the Jews' unlanded status and their work in handicrafts. Their distinct religious affiliation led to their being disenfranchised from ownership of agricultural land, which, in turn, forced them to work in artisanship, a very poorly regarded occupation in Ethiopia.

7. See, for example, Abbink (1987) and Krempel (1972).

8. See further Donham and James (1986: 5), Leslau (1951), and Simoons (1960: 29, 174–191).

9. Smithery has been linked with supernatural or magical powers as well as with Judaism in other cultures as well, some close to the Ethiopian (Africa) and others distant (Europe in certain periods). In these cases, too, the craft of the smith was viewed with ambivalence and often involved social isolation. For a detailed discussion on smithery, pottery, and belief systems in Africa, see Herbert (1993).

10. Simoons (1960: 180–181).

11. The term "eat" is the standard metaphorical image in Ethiopia for using the evil eye.

12. There is no documentation of Jewish landownership in Ethiopia (see Rosen [1987]), but it was mentioned in interviews with immigrants from these regions. They also spoke of the historical events that led to their being awarded the land.

13. See also Kaplan (1992a: 168).

CHAPTER 3.   THE JEW AS *BUDA*

1. See Honea (1956), Reminick (1973, 1976), and many others.

2. See also Abbink (1987) and Krempel (1972).

3. Although all the groups in the region shared the same general views regarding the magical forces at work in the world, and the magical categories in which the Jews were placed, the immigrants vehemently denied possessing supernatural powers.

4. See, for example, Honea (1956: 20–22), Messing (1975: 396), and Pankhurst (1990: 223–224).

5. On the hyena-man as a trans-African phenomenon, see, for example, Calame-Griaule and Ligers (1961), Dorson (1972), and Herbert (1993).

6. See also Abbink (1987), Kaplan (1987, 1992a), and Messing (1975). For a wider discussion on the evil eye and wet-dry categories, see Dundes (1980: 93–133).

7. At times, personal long-term ties developed between a certain artisan and his Christian clients, ties that might extend over several generations. In such an instance, these ties served as proof that the family did not put its magical powers to evil use.

8. See also Leslau (1964: 209).

9. We see here an interesting double connection. The smoke and the fire served as the most visual identifying marks of the Jews, because their work in crafts was associated so strongly with magical powers. The ability to control fire was perceived as one which requires supernatural powers, and it is through smoke and fire that the destructive power of this force can be stopped.

10. See Messing (1975: 395–396).

11. See also Messing (1975: 395).

12. See, for example, Dundes (1989).

13. See Geddes (1986) on "Various Children of Eve (AT758)" tale type.

14. Reminick (1973: 33–34).

15. See Frank (1994: 38–41).

16. Just as the Jews are distinguished from their Christian (hyena sibling) neighbors by their landness, so Cain, the original murderer and indeed the first sibling murderer, was fated with the punishment of eternal wandering. I wish to thank Doug Arava for suggesting this additional dimension to the parallel metaphor of competing brothers. See also Hasan-Rokem and Dundes (1985).

17. See Reminick (1973: 34).

CHAPTER 4. GIFT GIVING AND THE MULTIPLE MEANINGS OF KNIVES AND SHEEP

1. Every group ate meat slaughtered only by and for itself. We shall return to this issue in Chapter 10.

2. This network is characterized by a regional supragroup commitment, during which a clear spatial definition emerges of who belongs to this system. See also Salamon (1986).

3. Recall my Ethiopian friends' three gifts brought to my wedding in Israel.

4. The importance of gift giving as a continuing process of exchange and commitment has been central to anthropology ever since the seminal works by Malinowski (1922) and Mauss (1924).

5. This same emperor conducted the famous debate between Jewish and Christian religious leaders. I shall return to this debate in Chapter 9.

6. See, for example, Leach's *Funk and Wagnalls Standard Dictionary of Folklore Mythology and Legend* (1950: 584–585).

CHAPTER 5. CHRISTIAN HELP WITH JEWISH DEAD

1. Though not reported in literature, mutual participation in funereal ceremonies was extremely common.

2. See Salamon (1986: 84–87).

3. It is widely believed in Ethiopia that the period of limbo between death and burial is a dangerous time during which people are particularly susceptible to the evil powers of supernatural forces. Believers of all religions are susceptible and share the desire to conclude the funeral as quickly as possible.

4. The ritual of burning a red heifer survived only among Ethiopian Jews. No longer observed by other Jewish communities around the world, these laws of purity and impurity, which appear in the Bible (Numbers 19), are strictly adhered to by Beta Israel.

5. A possible reference to the *Kifu-qen* (the Terrible Era). This era is described by his informants as one of terrible famine when many Ethiopians, among them Jews, starved to death. This is also the time when other separating customs between the groups ceased being observed (Kaplan 1990b).

6. *Qesim* is the plural form of *qes* used very often by my informants when speaking to me. The suffix *-im* is the Hebrew plural suffix, while in Amharic the plural of most nouns is formed by adding *-och*, thus *Qesoch*.

CHAPTER 6. RELIGIOUS HOLIDAYS

1. Molvaer (1980: 64–65) states that the Ethiopians relied more on the "list" of holy days in establishing daily meetings than on the numerical dates. This was especially true in the more rural areas.

2. Emphases in italics throughout the interviewees' citations are mine (H. S.). The Christian calendar in Ethiopia is basically solar. It consists of 365 days, which are divided into twelve months of thirty days, with five or six additional days per year. Beta Israel use this calendar in their daily life but base their holidays on a lunar calendar. See, for example, Leslau (1951: xxviii–xxxvi; 1957) and Kaplan (1990a).

3. *Tabot* is the term for both the tablets of the law and the table which symbolizes them. It also serves as a common reference to the church and to a saint. See, for example, Molvaer (1980: 259).

4. On the existence—mainly in the past—of monks/hermits among the Beta Israel, see, for example, Ben Dor (1985b), Kaplan (1984, 1988), and Leslau (1975).

5. When talking to me, the speakers used the Hebrew word *pesel* ("statue") to describe icons of holy images in the Ethiopian church.

6. On the external appearance of the Torah in Ethiopia, see Leslau (1951: xxviii), and Figure 17.

7. On the Sigd, see Abbink (1983), Ben Dor (1985a), Salamon (1986: 62–68), and Shelemay (1989: 56), who remarks that " Sigd is . . . the most syncretist observance."

8. Goldberg's 1987 fascinating study, in which the Jewish Mimuna in Morocco is examined in the context of symbolic intergroup relations, is a good example of such analysis.

9. On the Sigd as a unique holiday for Ethiopian Jewry, see, for example, Abbink (1983), Ben Dor (1985a), and Salamon (1987: 62–68).

10. For these holidays, see Leslau (1951: xxix–xxxv).

11. Molvaer (1980: 95) describes similar gifts given by Christians to the church in times of supplication or oaths.

12. These requests may be seen as another expression of the "power of the weak," in which the weaker group, politically, is perceived as representing a general, super-religious human morality, or as maintaining contact with the forces of nature in such a way as to allow for the fulfillment of wishes. The weaker group is often sought out if it is viewed as being more fundamentally or originally tied to the place. On power strategies of weaker groups, see also Scott (1985, 1990). For an interesting comparison to the Jews in Muslim Morocco, see Rosen (1972).

13. The Israeli monetary unit. Used here to represent a metal coin.

14. See, for example, Kaplan (1992a: 162–163).

CHAPTER 7. THE TWICE-DISGUISED HYENA

1. See also Kaplan (1992a: 116–142).

2. The term "liminality" in this sense was developed by the anthropologist

Victor Turner (1967, 1969) and refers to the intermediate stage in transitional states.

3. An accepted typology in the literature of religious conversion distinguishes "recruitment" from "affiliation." This parallels the distinction Beta Israel are trying to establish in claiming that the conversion of Ethiopian Jews was only "recruitment." On religious conversions in Africa from a cultural perspective, see Colson (1970), Fisher (1973), Horton (1971, 1975a, 1975b), and Peel (1968, 1977).

4. On this issue, see also Messing (1971).

5. For a detailed list of the names for converted Jews used by Beta Israel in different regions, see Salamon (1994: 115–118). On the *feras mura* and the State of Israel, see the recent extensive study by Seemen (1997).

6. An interesting discussion is found in Levtzion (1990), who deals with different levels of conversion pressure applied by Muslims to Jews and Christians. The inequality is explained by the groups' different economic—not spiritual—level.

7. Schoenberger (1975: 37–38) and Messing (1971: 24).

8. The participation of converts in Sigd was also mentioned in Kaplan (1987).

9. For a similar case in which a Muslim sheikh in Ethiopia converted to Christianity and undertook missionary activity in Muslim villages, see Crummey (1972).

10. See, for example, Lord (1970) and Salamon (1986: 92–96). The "fixed site," that is, the grave, emphasized the fixed liminality of the converts and the impossibility of a full intergroup transformation.

11. Messing (1971: 23) and Abbink (1984: 65).

CHAPTER 8. FLESH AND BONES

1. Though slavery in Ethiopia was legally abolished in 1924 and its trade prohibited, slaves continued until very recently to form part of family property—they were subject to inheritance as part of an estate (see also Derrik [1975: 152], Flad [1869: 25], LeRoy [1979], Levine [1974: 56], McCann [1988], Messing [1957: 413–415; 1962: 386–408], and Rapoport [1980:19]). These (now former) slaves had emigrated with the Beta Israel to Israel. On the term *chewa*, meaning a free, civilized person, see Rosen (1985a: 56–57) and Crummey (1980: 121).

2. This statement reflected a strong desire to distance the *barya* both geographically and culturally.

3. See, for example, Schoenberger (1975: 72–73) and Rosen (1993).

4. This same historical-religious story appears in the *Kebra-Nagast*, the Ethiopian national epic. There the slaves are depicted as Ham's chastized progeny and the Amhara as the children of Shem, found worthy of rule. See also LeRoy (1979: 10). The informants explained the link between the slaves and the tribe of Ham by citing Genesis 9:25–28. For a discussion of the *Kebra-Nagast,* its sources and significance in Ethiopia, see Ullendorff (1968: 74–79).

5. See, for example, Leslau (1951: xxxvi) and Simoons (1960).

6. Beta Israel themselves underwent purification ceremonies at various stages

of ritual impurity. Though less strenuous than *barya* conversion (circumcision not being included), procedurally they were similar.

7. According to Numbers 21:1, Moses had a black Cushite wife. Some of the informants suggested a twofold connection here, though perhaps illogically, between marriage to a Cushite and circumcision in adulthood.

8. The following is a list of some of the popular names and their meanings according to the informants: *Tamasgan*—praise to God—"praise Him because He gave me a gift"; *Satai*—"God helped me" or "God gave me in order to help me"; *Desta*—joy, a name given not only to slaves but in this case meaning "now I am happy for I can sleep quietly and he will work in my place"; *Radai*—"helper"; *Agus*—"that which God gave me."

9. On this matter, see Salamon (1995a: 129–132).

10. Among the Beta Israel, in addition to the dichotomic *barya* / *chewa*, a free man is called *ivrawi* vis-à-vis the topic of slaves. This name relates to the *Orit* and to the interaction between Hebrews and slaves as described in sacred writ. The issue of two slaves was called *mo'olad-ouladg*, a person born of a *barya*. The master of a *barya* is sometimes referred to as *getau*, a title relating specifically to a *chewa* owner of a *barya*. Without going into too much detail, mixed children were generally known as *diqala* and *asherato*. *Diqala* is a general term for a bastard, according to Beta Israel interpretation of Pentateuchal laws. The informants explained that the same term could be used for the offspring of an unwed couple, though it was generally assumed to denote a child of mixed *barya-chewa* parentage. Such a child was also known by the the derogatory term of *asherato* (literally, a cross-breed of peas and beans). Neither group was specifically identified with one or the other elements of this idea. For a specific terminology defining the issue of such mixed parentage as far as an "eighth slave," see LeRoy (1979: 15). A detailed classification of specific terminology used by Ethiopian Christians is supplied by Pankhurst (1976) and Seifu (1972: 127–200). This phenomenon, of slaves remaining outsiders for many generations, is known in other cultural contexts as well. For another Judaic context, see Urbach (1988, especially 166).

11. See also Halévy (1877: 43–44).

12. Beta Israel monks only ate meat slaughtered by other monks and not by a *qes*, a *qes* could only eat meat slaughtered by another *qes*, and so on; see also Flad (1869).

13. Attempting to clarify the Ethiopian reality for me while being interviewed in Israel, the informants enlisted the term *kosher*. Concerning the Beta Israel religious dietary laws, see, for example, Leslau (1951).

14. The aim of the *tazkar* feast's *maswit* ritual is to help the soul of the deceased be admitted to heaven. The feast is celebrated by Beta Israel and Christians alike. See also Faitlovitch (1959: 53–54) and Shelemay (1989: 43).

CHAPTER 9. CRUCIFIERS AND IDOL MAKERS

1. See also Kapeliuk (1986: 341) and Levine (1965: 230–231).

2. Especially the writings of Flad (1869; 1922), Gobat (1850), and Stern (1968).

3. See also Kaplan (1992a: 125).

4. This particular dispute is mentioned by Ben Dor (1993), Halévy (1906), Kaplan (1992a: 130–131), and Leslau (1947).

5. One cannot ignore the strong bond between church and state in Ethiopia as a partial explanation for sublimation via the *haymanot* (see, for example, Sergew [1972] and Taddesse [1972]).

6. The term "master" is used here due to its doubly appropriate meaning: "to control" and as "unlocking all doors." See also "Master Narrative," in Jameson (1981).

7. On the complexity of identity and otherness in Ethiopian context, see, for example, Pawlikowski (1972) and Ullendorff (1968).

8. The Quran in Ethiopia is written in Arabic.

9. According to research on missionaries among the Beta Israel, this crime was central to the missionaries' arguments. These missionaries, interestingly, were among the first to describe the Beta Israel as part of world Jewry. See Kaplan (1992a: ch. 6, especially 138–142).

CHAPTER 10. OUR BLOOD, THEIR BLOOD

1. See, for example, Turner on blood as a primordial symbol (1967: 28; 1977), and also Buckley and Gottlieb (1988).

2. On the "covenant of blood" in Rabbinic Judaism, see Hoffman (1996).

3. On blood as a "core symbol," see also Wagner (1986: 96–125). For discussion and elaboration of the term, see Ortner (1973).

4. Consider in this context their skepticism concerning the actual paternity of Jesus.

5. The level of overlapping between the symbolic systems are, in this case, greater than that found in many other examples. An additional point is the dichotomy between pure and impure. Without going into too much detail, I will only mention that for the Beta Israel, purity is understood as the inverse of impurity, but at the same time there are many subcategories of the two states which require concrete, contextual exploration.

6. Note the double nature of these statements, in which every description of a Jewish custom is accompanied by a description of a corresponding Christian one.

7. For this discussion, see also Rosen (1981: 46). In her reference to a different cultural context (North African Jewish women), Rosen points to the strong element of Jewish identity inherent in going to the *mikve*. She writes that "blood makes a woman out of a girl, and the *mikve* makes a Jewess out of a woman."

8. On the usage of similar images and idioms between proximate Ethiopian groups, the Amhara and the Dassenetch, see Almagor (1986: 108).

9. See also Leslau (1951: xx).

10. See, for example, the entry on "blood" in Eliade (1986).

11. See Richardson (1977).

12. Another example can be found in the Gojam region of Ethiopia, where the term "Damenenza" was a synonym for the Falasha, meaning "let His blood be on them" (Kaplan [1990a: 154]).

13. On sacrifice among the Beta Israel in Ethiopia, see Lifchitz (1939: 116–123). For two extremely relevant and sophisticated discussions, see Feeley-Harnik (1981: especially ch. 5) and Dundes (1989) on blood libel legends and anti-Semitism in other cultural contexts.

14. For an elaborated discussion on the "covenant of blood" in Judaism, especially in the rabbinic period of the first two or three centuries C.E., see Hoffman (1996).

15. On the cooked / raw opposition as an expression of the boundaries between human and inhuman (civilized / uncivilized), see Levi-Strauss (1969).

16. See also Abbink (1987). There were those who spoke of the eating of the blood of dead Jewish children. When they were asked why only children, they explained that children were pure of sin. The same explanation was given for the eating of the blood of converts, i.e., Beta Israel who became Christians. These people were considered clean of sin.

17. See Dundes' "Projective Inversion" argument (1989:16–18).

18. Similar expressions, at the end of the previous century, are cited by Halévy (1877: 43). Another study, dealing with the relations between the Amhara and the Dassenetch in Ethiopia, mentions a central image in which the Dassenetch describe the Amhara as "people who eat raw meat." Interestingly, this same image became central for both the Dassenetch and the Beta Israel in relation to the Christian Amhara. The perceptions which stand behind the two images are, nevertheless, very different, for the Beta Israel interpreted this image according to written Biblical law.

19. On group boundaries, identity, and food taboos, see Douglas (1966).

CHAPTER 11. THE BATTLE OF METAPHORS

1. *Dohoné* or *dehono*, as it is sometimes pronounced, is described in Kane's dictionary as "a sort of bowl made of a mixture of cow dung and chaff" (Kane [1990: 1704]).

2. Beck (1978: 84). On metaphors and cultural understanding, see also Fernandez (1974: 123; 1977, 1991b), Quinn (1991), Srivastva and Barrett (1988), and the entire important book on the theory of tropes in anthropology edited by Fernandez (1991a).

3. Davis (1975: 234).

4. See Hasan-Rokem (1982), Herzog and Blooah (1936), Kirshenblatt-Gimblett (1973), and Seitel (1977). For further elaboration of the theoretical aspects of the subject, see Salamon (1995a).

5. See, for example, Briggs (1988), Kirshenblatt-Gimblett (1973), Roberts and Hayes (1987), and Seitel (1977), and with specific attention to the interaction between structure and context, Hasan-Rokem (1982). For a comprehensive discussion of context in the study of folklore, see Ben Amos (1993). The present discussion is indebted to the contributions of Kirkmann (1984; 1985), Jason (1971), Norrick (1985), and especially Lieber, in his important paper on "Analogic Ambiguity: A Paradox of Proverb Usage" (1984).

6. The term was first suggested by Schon (1979), in his paper on "generative metaphor," but in a slightly different sense from that used here.

7. See Pepper (1942) for "root metaphors," Turner (1967; 1977) for a discussion of "dominant symbols," Wagner (1986) on "trope," Fernandez (1991a; 1991b: 5) on "Organizing Metaphor," and Ortner's "On Key Symbols" (1973) for a systematic discussion of the subject.

8. In this connection, see Fernandez (1973: 1366) and Maltz (1978: 29).

9. On this matter, see Leslau (1951: xiii).

10. Ibid.

11. See, for example, Messing (1971) and Simoons (1960: 28).

12. As Christians very often bought their metal crucifixes from the Beta Israel blacksmiths, this of course strengthened the Beta Israel's argument that "the Christians pray to an object made by us."

13. This is the term used by the Beta Israel informants. Interestingly, its meaning almost exactly parallels the English expression "half-baked."

14. In Jewish religious literature, see for example the Babylonian Talmud, Tractate Sanhedrin 39b: "The axe handle comes from the forest." Compare also the traditional interpretation of Isaiah 49:17, "Thy destroyers and ravagers from thee shall go forth." For a parallel in the classical tradition, compare Aesop's fable of the eagle impaled by an arrow made of its own feather.

15. This was the case, even though the word "Christian" was not used in these interpretations and the dohoné-Christian identification was not obvious in this proverb. In the course of the interviews, the informants seemed to take special pride in this proverb and in their interpretations of it. The Beta Israel's pride in this case parallels the methods of camouflage developed in other aspects of life.

16. It is possible to view this as the anthropomorphization of the different religions and the use of terms drawn from family life to describe the relations between them.

17. On the uses and meanings of expressive features (folkloric forms or genres) in connection with the social realm in African society, see also Ben Amos (1975).

18. For an interesting discussion on interpretation, see the "Introduction" in Briggs (1988).

CHAPTER 12. TRANSFORMATIONS

1. See, for example, Herbert's *Iron, Gender and Power* (1993).

2. Sperber's *Rethinking Symbolism* (1975) presents a cultural structure that reproduces and transfers basic cultural dichotomies highly relevant for the present discussion. See also, Levi-Strauss (1966).

3. For a discussion of this issue preceding the case of Ethiopian Jews and their immigration to Israel, see Patai (1975).

Glossary

ABBA "father," title of respect

AGAW early Cushitic-speaking population of Ethiopian highlands; also used as a general designation for "pagan" groups, applied derogatorily to Ethiopian Jews

AMHARA Amharic-speaking people dominant politically since the thirteenth century; also synonym for "Christian"

AMLAK YISRAEL "king of Israel"

ARBATOM "four fasts," a Christian religious observance

ASHERATO mixed children of *chewa* and *barya*

ATTINKUGN LAWS Beta Israel purity laws

BARYA "slave," referring to both origin and status

BET-QEDDUS prayer house

BET-TSELOT prayer house

BETA ISRAEL "House of Israel," term preferred by Ethiopian Jews when referring to themselves while in Ethiopia

BILLAWA personal knife, similar to a pocketknife, often given as a gift by Jews to Christians

BUDA magical concept of hyena-man, derogatory appellation applied to Beta Israel

CHEWA term designating free man (as opposed to *barya*), possessor of *barya;* also refers to a civilized, educated person

DAS open hut usually built for ceremonies

DIB a bear

DIQALA general term for bastard; also used for offspring of a*barya–chewa* liaison

DOHONÉ (DEHONO) vessel made of mud mixed with straw, insulting code word referring to Christians

EGZIABEHAR God

FALASHA appellation for Beta Israel, viewed by them as uncomplimentary

FELASMUQRA Jews converted to Christianity

FELASMURA Jews converted to Christianity

FERANJ "stranger," used to designate white people

GE'EZ ancient Ethiopic, language of both Jewish and Christian sacred writings and prayers

GOMA "smoke," used to exorcise "evil eye" powers

HAYMANOT the totality of beliefs and practices of any religious tradition

INJERA Ethiopian "bread," made from indigenous grain

JIB " hyena," offensive appellation for Beta Israel

JIRATAM "tail," offensive appellation for Beta Israel linked to the image of the *buda*

KARA curved knife

KAYLA pejorative appellation for Beta Israel

KEBRA-NAGAST Ethiopian national epic

MAREJIYA KARA straight knife

MASGID prayer house

MASWIT responsive chanting of prayers for the soul of the departed

MELEKUSE monks

MES'HAF QEDDUS "Holy Book," scripture

MESQEL crucifix

MO'OLAD-OULADG offspring of *barya* ancestry

ORIT Ge'ez translation of Old Testament

QABER burial

QABER BET "house of burial," cemetery

QES priest, term used for both Beta Israel and Christians

SEGAW WADEMU "His flesh and His blood"

SIGD holiday of fasting and prayer unique to Beta Israel

TABOT tablets of the law and the table symbolizing them

TAZKAR remembrance day, a rite to raise the soul of the deceased

TEBIB (AN) from Ge'ez *tabba*, to be skilled, appellation with derogatory connotation referring to artisans, especially crafts tinged with supernatural powers

TEF grain typical of Ethiopia, usually used for *injera*

temqat baptism

TELLA beer usually made from barley

WANGEL New Testament, the Gospels (evangel)

YAMARGAM GOJO "hut of the curse," hut for Beta Israel women during menstruation or postpartum periods

YEDEM BET "house of blood," hut for Beta Israel women during menstruation or postpartum periods

YEDEM GOJO "blood hut," hut for Beta Israel women during menstruation or postpartum periods

YUDIT (GUDITH) principal Beta Israel female leader prominent in the group's ethnohistorical stories

ZAGWA name of the Christian Agaw dynasty

References

d'Abbadie, A. 1851–52. "Réponses des falashas dit juif d'Abyssinie aux questions faites par M. Luzzato." *Archives israélites*, 12: 179–185, 234–240, 259–269.

Abbink, G. J. 1983. "Seged Celebrations in Ethiopia and Israel: Continuity and Change of a Falasha Religious Holiday." *Anthropos*, 78: 789–810.

———. 1984. "The Falasha in Ethiopia and Israel: The Problem of Ethnic Assimilation." *Nijmegen Sociaal Anthropologische Cahiers*, 15.

———. 1987. "A Socio-Structural Analysis of the Beta-Esra'el as an 'Infamous Group' in Traditional Ethiopia." *Sociologus*, 39 (4): 140–154.

———. 1990. "The Enigma of Beta Esraél Ethnogenesis: An Ethnohistorical Study." *Cahiers d'études africaines*, 30 (120): 392–449.

Aešcoly, A. Z. 1943. *The Book of the Falasha*. Tel Aviv: Masada. (Hebrew)

Almagor, U. 1986. "Institutionalizing a Fringe Periphery: Dassanetch–Amhara Relations." In D. Donham and W. James, eds., *The Southern Marches of Imperial Ethiopia*, pp. 96–115. Cambridge: Cambridge University Press.

Bahloul, J. 1996. *The Architecture of Memory*. Cambridge: Cambridge University Press.

Beck, B. E. F. 1978. "The Metaphor as a Mediator Between Semantic and Analogic Modes of Thought." *Current Anthropology*, 19(1): 83–88.

Ben Amos, D. 1975. "Folklore in African Society." *Research in African Literature*, 6(2): 165–198.

———. 1993. "'Context' in Context." *Western Folklore*, 52: 209–226.

Ben Dor, S. 1985a. "Ha'sigd shel Beta Israel: Hag hidush ha'brith." M.A. thesis, Hebrew University of Jerusalem. (Hebrew)

———. 1985b. "The Holy Places of Ethiopian Jewry." *Pe'amim*, 22: 32–52. (Hebrew)

———. 1987. "The Religious Life of Ethiopian Jews." In Y. Avner et al., eds., *Beta Israel: The Story of Ethiopian Jewry*, pp. 58–63. Tel-Aviv: Beth Hatefutsoth. (Hebrew)

———. 1993. "The Ties Between the Jews of Ethiopia and the Emperor Tewo-dros." *Pe'amim*, 58: 67–85. (Hebrew)

Boyarin, J. 1991. *Polish Jews in Paris: The Ethnography of Memory.* Blooming-ton: Indiana University Press.

———. 1998. "Martyrdom and the Making of Christianity and Judaism." *Journal of Christian Studies*, 6 (4): 557–627.

———. 1999. *Dying for God: Martyrdom and the Making of Christianity and Judaism.* Stanford: Stanford University Press.

Brandes, S. H. 1980. *Metaphors of Masculinity.* Philadelphia: University of Penn-sylvania Press.

Briggs, C. L. 1988. *Competence in Performance.* Philadelphia: University of Penn-sylvania Press.

Bruce, J. 1805. *Travels to Discover the Sources of the Nile.* 2nd ed. Edinburgh: Cambridge University Press.

Buckley, T., and A. Gottlieb, eds. 1988. *Blood Magic: The Anthropology of Men-struation.* Berkeley: University of California Press.

Budge, Sir E. A. W. 1928. *A History of Ethiopia, Nubia and Abyssinia.* Doster-hout: N. B. Anthropological Publications.

Buxton, D. 1970. *The Abyssinians.* New York: Praeger.

Calame-Griaule, G., and Ligers, Z. 1961. "L'homme-hyène dans la tradition soudanaise." *L'homme*, 1: 89–118.

Cerulli, E. 1956. *Storia della letteratura etiopica.* Milan: Nuova Accademia Editrice.

Chelouche, D. 1988. *The Exiles of Israel Will Be Gathered.* Jerusalem: Achva. (Hebrew)

Colson, E. 1970. "Converts and Tradition: The Impact of Christianity on Val-ley Tonga Religion." *Southwestern Journal of Anthropology*, 26: 143–156.

Conti Rossini, C. 1928. *Storia d'Etiopia.* Bergamo: Instituto Italiano d'Arti Grafiche.

———. 1937. *Etiopia e Genti di Etiopia*, pp. 136, 200–202. Edited by R. and F. Bemporan. Firenze.

Cooper, F. 1979. "Review Article: The Problem of Slavery in African Studies." *Journal of African History*, 20 (1): 103–125.

Corinaldi, M. 1988. *Ethiopian Jewry—Identity and Tradition.* Jerusalem: Ru-bin Mass. (Hebrew)

Crummey, D. 1972. "Sheikh Zakaryas: An Ethiopian Prophet." *Journal of Ethiopian Studies*, 10 (1): 56–66.

———. 1980. "Abyssinian Feudalism." *Past and Present*, 89: 115–138.

Davis, N. Z. 1975. *Society and Culture in Early Modern France.* Stanford: Stan-ford University Press.

Derrik, W. 1975. *Africa's Slaves Today.* London.

Donham, D., and W. James., eds. 1986. *The Southern Marches of Imperial Ethio-pia.* Cambridge: Cambridge University Press.

Dorson, R. M . 1972. "Africa and the Folklorist." In R. Dorson, ed., *African Folklore*, pp. 3–67. Bloomington: Indiana University Press.

Douglas, M. 1966. *Purity and Danger: An Analysis of Concepts of Pollution and Taboo.* London: Routledge & Kegan Paul.

Dundes, A. 1980. "Wet and Dry, the Evil Eye: An Essay in Indo-European and Semitic Worldview." In A. Dundes, ed., *Interpreting Folklore*, pp. 93–133. Bloomington: Indiana University Press.

———. 1989. "The Ritual Murder or Blood Libel Legend: A Study of Anti-Semitic Victimization through Projective Inversion." *Temenos*, 25: 7–32.

Eliade, M., ed. 1986. *The Encyclopedia of Religion*. New York: Macmillan.

Faitlovitch, J. 1905. *Notes d'un voyage chez les falachas (juifs d'Abyssinie)*. Paris: Leroux.

———. 1959 (1910). *Journey to the Falasha*. Tel Aviv: Devir. (Hebrew)

Feeley-Harnik, G. 1981. *The Lord's Table*. Philadelphia: University of Pennsylvania Press.

Fernandez, J. W. 1973. "Analysis of Ritual: Metamorphic Correspondence as the Elementary Forms." *Science* 182 (4119): 1366–1367.

———. 1974. "The Mission of Metaphor in Expressive Culture." *Current Anthropology*, 15(2): 119–144.

———. 1977. "The Performance of Ritual Metaphors." In J. D. Sapir and J. C. Crocker, eds., pp. 100–131. *The Social Use of Metaphor*. Philadelphia: University of Pennsylvania Press.

———. 1991a. *Beyond Metaphor: The Theory of Tropes in Anthropology*. Stanford: Stanford University Press.

———. 1991b. "Introduction: Confluents of Inquiry." In J. W. Fernandez, ed., *Beyond Metaphor: The Theory of Tropes in Anthropology*, pp. 1–13. Stanford: Stanford University Press.

Fischer, M. 1986. "Ethnicity and the Post-Modern Arts of Memory." In J. Clifford and G. Marcus, eds., *Writing Culture*, pp. 194–233. Berkeley: University of California Press.

Fisher, H. J. 1973. "Conversion Reconsidered: Some Historical Aspects of Religious Conversion in Black Africa." *Africa*, 43: 27–44.

Flad, J. M. 1869. *The Falashas (Jews) of Abissinia*. Translated by S. P. Goodhart. London: William Macintosh.

———. 1922. *60 Jahre in der Mission unter den Falachas in Abyssinien*. Giesen: Brunnen.

Frank, L. 1994. "When Hyenas Kill Their Own." *New Scientist*, 5 (March): 38–41.

Gamst, F. 1969. *The Qemant: A Pagan-Hebraic Peasantry of Ethiopia*. New York: Holt, Rinehart and Winston.

Geddes, V. G. 1986. "Various Children of Eve (AT758): Cultural Variants and Antifeminine Images." *Ethnolore* (Uppsala), 5.

Geertz, C. 1988. *Works and Lives: The Anthropologist as Author*. Stanford: Stanford University Press.

Gobat, S. 1850. *Journal of a Three Years' Residence in Abysinnia*. 2nd ed. London.

Goldberg, H. 1978. "The Mimuna and the Minority Status of Moroccan Jews." *Ethnology*, 17: 75–87.

———. 1992. "Potential Polities: Jewish Saints in the Moroccan Countryside and in Israel." In M. Bax, P. Kloos, and A. Koster, eds., *Faith and Polity: Essays on Religion and Politics*, pp. 235–250. Amsterdam: Vrije Universiteit University Press.

Goody, J. 1980. "Slavery in Time and Space." In J. L. Watson, ed., *Asian and African Systems of Slavery*, pp. 16–22. Berkeley: University of California Press.

Griaule, M. 1934–1935. "L'esclavage en Abyssinie." *Etudes de sociologie et d'ethnologie juridiques*, 21: 23–43.

Halévy, J. 1877. "Halévy's Travels in Abyssinia." In *Miscellany of Hebrew Literature*, pp. 5–80. London: Wertheimer, Lea.

———. 1906. "La guerre de Sarsa—Dengel contre les falasha, extrait des Annales de Sarsa-Dengel." *Revue sémitique*, 14: 392–427; 15: 119–163, 263–287.

Hasan-Rokem, G. 1982. *Proverbs in Israeli Folk Narratives: A Structural Semantic Analysis*. Folklore Fellows Communications, No. 232. Helsinki: Academia Scientiarum Fennica.

———. 1996. *The Web of Life: Folklore in Rabbinic Judaism*. Tel-Aviv: Am Oved. (Hebrew)

Hasan-Rokem, G., and A. Dundes., eds. 1985. *The Wandering Jew: Essays in the Interpretation of Christian Legend*. Bloomington: Indiana University Press.

Herbert, E. W. 1993. *Iron, Gender and Power: Rituals of Transformation in African Societies*. Bloomington: Indiana University Press.

Herzog, G., and C. Blooah. 1936. *Jabo Proverbs from Liberia*. Oxford: Oxford University Press/ International Institute of African Language and Culture.

Hess, R. I. 1969. "Toward a History of the Falasha." In D. F. McCall, N. R. Bennett, and J. Butler, eds. *Eastern African History*, pp. 107–132. Boston University Papers on Africa, No. 3. New York: Praeger.

Hoben, A. 1970. "Social Stratification in Traditional Amhara Society." In A. Tuden and L. Plotnicov, eds., *Social Stratification in Africa*, pp. 187–224. New York: Free Press.

———. 1973. *Land Tenure Among the Amhara of Ethiopia*. Chicago: University of Chicago Press.

Hoffman, L. A. 1996. *Covenant of Blood: Circumcision and Gender in Rabbinic Judaism*. Chicago: Chicago University Press.

Honea, K. 1956. "Buda in Ethiopia." In *Wiener völkerkundliche Mitteilungen*, 4(1): 20–24.

Horton, R. 1971. "African Conversion." *Africa*, 41: 85–108.

———. 1975a. "On the Rationality of Conversion." *Africa*, 45: 219–235.

———. 1975b. "On the Rationality of Conversion (part 2)." *Africa*, 45:373–399.

Jameson, F. 1981. *The Political Unconscious*. London: Methuen.

Jason, H. 1971. "The Approach of Russian Formalism and Its Western Followers to Oral Literature: A Critical Survey." *Ha-sifrut*, 3: 53–84. (Hebrew)

Kane, T. L. 1990. *Amharic-English Dictionary*. Wiesbaden: Otto Harrassowitz.

Kapeliuk, O. 1986. "Pseudo-questions in Amharic." In *Sixth International Conference of Ethiopian Studies*, pp. 337–341. Rotterdam and Boston: A. A. Balkema.

Kaplan, S. 1984. *The Monastic Holy Man and the Christianization of Early Solomonic Ethiopia*. Wiesbaden: F. Steiner.

———. 1987. "The Beta Israel (Falasha) Encounter with Protestant Missionaries: 1860–1905." *Jewish Social Studies*, 49(1): 27–42.

———. 1988. "Leadership and Communal Organization Among the Beta Israel

(Falasha): An Historical Study." *Encyclopedia Judaica Yearbook 1986–7*, pp. 154–163. Jerusalem: Keter.

———. 1989. "The Literature of the Beta Israel: Retrospect and Prospect." *Pe'amim*, 41: 90–111. (Hebrew)

———. 1990a. *Les falashas*. Turnhout, Belgium: Brepols.

———. 1990b. "Kifu-Qen: The Great Famine of 1888–1892 and the Beta Israel (Falasha)." *Paideuma*, 36: 67–77.

———. 1992a. *The Beta-Israel (Falasha) in Ethiopia: From Earliest Times to the Twentieth Century*. New York: New York University Press.

———. 1992b. "Indigenous Categories and the Study of World Religions in Ethiopia: The Case of the Beta-Israel (Falasha)." *Journal of Religion in Africa*, 22(3): 208–221.

Kaplan, S., and S. Ben Dor, eds. 1988. *Ethiopian Jewry: An Annotated Bibliography*. Jerusalem: Ben-Zvi Institute.

Kaplan, S., and H. Rosen 1993. "Ethiopian Immigrants in Israel: Between Preservation of Culture and Invention of Tradition." *Jewish Journal of Sociology*, 35 (1): 35–48.

Kessler, D. 1982. *The Falashas—The Forgotten Jews of Ethiopia*. New York: Africana.

Kirkman, A. 1984. "On Denotative Indefiniteness of Proverbs." *Proverbium*, 1: 47–91.

———. 1985. "Some Additional Aspects of Semantic Indefiniteness of Proverbs" *Proverbium*, 2: 58–85.

Kirshenblatt-Gimblett, B. 1973. "Toward a Theory of Proverb Meaning." *Proverbium*, 22: 821–827.

Krempel, V., 1972. "Die Soziale und wirtchaftliche Stellung der Falascha in der christlich-amharischen wirtchaftliche von Nordwest-Athiopien." Ph.D. dissertation. Frein Universitat, Berlin.

———. 1974. "Eine Berufskaste in Nordwest Athiopien—die Kayla (Falascha)." *Sociologus*, 24: 37–55.

Lamar-Ross, E. 1978. "Interethnic Communication: An Overview." In E. Lamar-Ross, ed., *Interethnic Communication*, pp. 1–13. Atlanta: University of Georgia Press.

Leach, M., ed. 1950. *Funk and Wagnalls Standard Dictionary of Folklore Mythology*. New York: Funk and Wagnalls.

LeRoy, P. E. 1979. "Slavery in the Horn of Africa." *Horn of Africa*, 2 (3): 10–19.

Leslau, W. 1947. "A Falasha Religious Dispute." *Proceedings of the American Academy for Jewish Research*, 16: 71–95.

———. 1951. *Falasha Anthology*. Yale Judaica Series, No. 6. New Haven: Yale University Press.

———. 1957. *Coutumes et croyances des falachas (juifs d'Abyssinie)*. Paris: Institute d'Ethnologie.

———. 1964. "An Ethiopian Argot of People Possessed by a Spirit." *Journal of Semitic Studies*, 9(1): 204–212.

———. 1975. "Taamrat Emanuel's Notes of Falasha Monks and Holy Places." In *Salo Wittmayer Baron Jubilee Volume*, pp. 623–637. Jerusalem: American Academy for Jewish Research.

Levi-Strauss, C. 1966. *The Savage Mind*. Chicago: University of Chicago Press.
————. 1969. *The Raw and the Cooked*. New York: Harper and Row.
Levine, D. N. 1965. *Wax and Gold*. Chicago: University of Chicago Press.
————. 1974. *Greater Ethiopia—The Evolution of a Multiethnic Society*. Chicago: University of Chicago Press.
Levtzion, N. 1990. "Conversions and Islamicization in the Middle Ages: How Did Jews and Christians Differ?" *Pe'amim*, 42: 8–15. (Hebrew)
Lieber, M. D. 1984. "Analogic Ambiguity: A Paradox of Proverb Usage." *Journal of American Folklore*, 97: 423–441. Reprinted in W. Mieder, ed., *Wise Words: Essays on the Proverb*, pp. 99–126. Garland Folklore Case Books, No. 6. New York: Garland.
Lifchitz, D. 1939. "Un sacrifice chez les falachas, juifs d'Abyssinie." *La terre et la vie*, 9: 116–123.
Lipsky, G. A. 1962. *Ethiopia—Its People, Its Society, Its Culture*. New Haven: Harf Press.
Loeb, L. D. 1977. *Outcaste—Jewish Life in Southern Iran*. New York: Gordon and Breach.
Lord, E. 1970. *Queen of Sheba's Heirs*. Washington, DC: Acropolis Books.
Malinowski, B. 1922. *Argonauts of the Western Pacific*. New York: Dutton.
Maltz, D. N. 1978. "The Bride of Christ Is Filled with His Spirit." In J. Hock-Smith and A. Spring, eds., *Women in Ritual and Symbolic Roles*, pp. 27–44. New York: Plenum Press.
Mauss, M. 1969 (1924). *The Gift*. London: Routledge & Kegan Paul.
McCann, J. 1988. "'Children of the House': Slavery and Its Suppression in Lasta, Northern Ethiopia, 1915–1935." In S. Miers and R. Roberts, eds., *End of Slavery in Africa*, pp. 332–361. Madison: University of Wisconsin Press.
Messing, S. D. 1957. "The Highland-Plateau of Ethiopia." Ph.D. dissertation. University of Pennsylvania.
————. 1962. "The Abyssinian Market Town." In P. Bohannan and G. Dalton, eds., *Markets in Africa*, pp. 386–408. Evanston, IL: Northwestern University Press.
————. 1971. "50,000 Black Marranos." *Jewish Heritage*, 13: 22–24.
————. 1975. "Health Care, Ethnic Outcasting, and the Problem of Overcoming the Syndrome of Encapsulation in a Peasant Society." *Human Organization*, 34 (4): 395–397.
————. 1982. *The Story of the Falashas—Black Jews of Ethiopia*. Brooklyn: Balshon Printing and Offset.
Molvaer, R. K. 1980. *Tradition and Change in Ethiopia*. Leiden: Brill.
Norrick, N. 1985. *How Proverbs Mean: Semantic Studies in English Proverbs*. Amsterdam: Mouton.
Ortner, S. 1973. "On Key Symbols." *American Anthropologist*, 75: 1338–1346.
Pankhurst, R. 1976. "The History of Bareya Sanquella and Other Ethiopian Slaves from the Borderlands of the Sudan." Unpublished paper presented to the Conference on Ethiopian Feudalism, Addis Ababa.
————. 1990. *A Social History of Ethiopia*. Addis Ababa: Institute of Ethiopian Studies, Addis Ababa University.
————. 1995. "The Béta Esra'él (Falashas) in Their Ethiopian Setting." *Israel*

Social Science Research 10(2): 1–12.

Patai, R. 1975. *The Myth of the Jewish Race,* New York: Scribners.

Peel, J. D. Y. 1968. "Syncretism and Religious Change." *Comparative Studies in Society and History,* 10: 121–141.

———. 1977. "Conversion and Tradition in Two African Societies: Ijebu and Buganda." *Past and Present,* 77: 108–141.

Pepper, S. C. 1942. *World Hypotheses.* Berkeley: University of California Press.

Pollera, A. 1940. *L'Abissinia di ieri.* Rome.

Quinn, N. 1991. "The Cultural Basis of Metaphor." In J. W. Fernandez, ed., *Beyond Metaphor: The Theory of Tropes in Anthropology,* pp. 56–93. Stanford: Stanford University Press.

Quirin, J. A. 1977. "The 'Beta Israel' (Falashas) in Ethiopian History: Caste Formation and Culture Change, 1868–1970." Ph.D. thesis. University of Minnesota.

———. 1992. *The Evolution of Ethiopian Jews: A History of the Beta Israel (Falasha) to 1920.* Philadelphia: University of Pennsylvania Press.

Rapoport, L. 1981. *The Lost Jews: Last of the Ethiopian Falashas.* New York: Stein and Day.

Rathjens, C. 1921. *Die Juden in Abessinien.* Hamburg: M. W. Kaufman.

Reminick, R. A. 1973. "The Structure and Functions of Religious Belief Among the Amhara of Ethiopia." In H. G. Marcus, ed., *Proceedings of the First United States Conference on Ethiopian Studies,* pp. 25–42. East Lansing: Michigan State University Press.

———. 1976. "The 'Evil Eye' Among the Amhara of Ethiopia." In C. Maloney, ed., *The Evil Eye,* pp. 85- 101. New York: Columbia University Press.

Richardson, A., ed. 1977. *A Dictionary of Christian Theology,* pp. 37–38. London: SCM Press.

Roberts, J. M., and J. C. Hayes. 1987. "Young Adults Male Categorization of Fifty Arabic Proverbs." *Anthropological Linguistics,* 29(1): 35–48.

Rosen, H. 1985a. "Core Symbols of Ethiopia Identity and Their Role in Understanding the Beta Israel Today." *Israel Social Science Research,* 3 (1–2): 55–62.

———. 1985b. "Falasha, Kayla, Beta-Israel? Ethnographic Observations on the Names for the Jews of Ethiopia." *Pe'amim,* 22: 53–58. (Hebrew)

———. 1987. "Similarities and Differences Between the Beta Israel of Gondar and Tigre." *Pe'amim,* 33: 93–108. (Hebrew)

———. 1993. "The Use of Genealogy among Beta Israel—On the Image of an Historical Hero in Literature and Oral Traditions." *Pe'amim,* 58: 120–128. (Hebrew)

Rosen, L. 1972. "Muslim-Jewish Relations in a Moroccan City." *International Journal of Middle Eastern Studies,* 3: 435–449.

Rosen, R. 1981. "Le symbolisme féminin ou la femme dans le système de représentation judeo-marocain, dans un mochav en Israel." M.A. thesis. Hebrew University of Jerusalem. (Hebrew)

Salamon, H. 1986. "Contacts and Communication Among the Beta-Israel in Ethiopia: Regional Aspects." M.A. thesis. Hebrew University of Jerusalem. (Hebrew)

———. 1987. "Journeys as a Means of Communication Among the Beta-Israel in Ethiopia." *Pe'amim*, 33, 1986. (Hebrew).

———. 1993. "Between Ethnicity and Religiosity: Internal Group Aspects of Conversion Among the Beta Israel in Ethiopia." *Pe'amim*, 58: 104–119. (Hebrew)

———. 1995a. "Metaphors as Corrective Exegesis: Three Proverbs of the Beta Israel." *Proverbium* 12: 295–313.

———. 1995b. "Reflections of Ethiopian Cultural Patterns on the 'Beta Israel' Absorption in Israel: The 'Barya' Case." In S. Kaplan, T. Parfitt and E. Trevisan-Semi, eds., *"Between Africa and Zion": Proceedings of the First International Conference on Ethiopian Jewry, Venice, 1993*, pp. 126–132. Jerusalem: Ben-Zvi Institute.

Salamon, H., and S. Kaplan. 1998. *Ethiopian Jewry: An Annotated Bibliography 1988–1997*. Jerusalem: Ben-Zvi Institute.

Schoenberger, M. 1975. "The Falashas of Ethiopia—an Ethnographic Study." M.A. thesis. Cambridge University.

Schon, D. A. 1979. "Generative Metaphor: A Perspective on Problem Solving in Social Policy." In A. Ortony, ed., *Metaphor and Thought*, pp. 254–283. Cambridge: Cambridge University Press.

Scott, J. C. 1985. *Weapons of the Weak: Everyday Forms of Peasant Resistance*. New Haven: Yale University Press.

———. 1990. *Domination and the Arts of Resistance: Hidden Transcripts*. New Haven: Yale University Press.

Seemen, D. F. 1997. "One People, One Blood: Religious Conversion, Public Health, and the Immigration as Social Experience for Ethiopian Jews." Ph.D. thesis submitted to Harvard University.

Seifu, M. F. 1972. "Terminology for 'Servant' (Slave?) in Amharic Tradition." *Journal of Ethiopian Studies*, 10(2): 127–200. (Amharic)

Seitel, P. 1977. "Saying Haya Sayings: Two Categories of Proverbs Use." In D. J. Sapir and C. Crocker, eds., *The Social Use of Metaphor*, pp. 75–99. Philadelphia: University of Pennsylvania Press.

Sergew, H. S. 1972. *Ancient and Medieval Ethiopian History to 1270*. Addis Ababa: United Printers.

Shack, W. A. 1974. *The Central Ethiopians: Amhara, Tigrina and Related Peoples*. London: International African Institute.

Sheba, C., Adam, A., and Bat-Miriam, M. 1962. "A Survey of Some Genetical Characters in Some Ethiopian Tribes." *American Journal of Physical Anthropology*, 20: 168–208.

Shelemay, K. K. 1989. *Music, Ritual and Falasha History*. East Lansing: Michigan State University Press/African Studies Center.

Simoons, F. J. 1960. *Northwest Ethiopia: People and Economy*. Madison: University of Wisconsin Press.

Sperber, D. 1975. *Rethinking Symbolism*. Cambridge: Cambridge University Press.

Srivastva, S., and Barrett, F. J. 1988. "The Transforming Nature of Metaphors in Group Development: A Study in Group Theory." *Human Relations*, 41(1): 31–64.

Stern, H. A. 1968. *Wanderings Among the Falashas in Abyssinia.* 2nd ed. London: Frank Cass.

Summerfield, D. P. 1997. "From Falashas to Ethiopian Jews: The External Influences for Change, C. 1860–1960." Ph.D. thesis submitted to the University of London.

Taddesse, T. 1972. *Church and State in Ethiopia: 1270–1527.* Oxford: Clarendon Press.

———. 1988. "Processes of Ethnic Interaction and Integration in Ethiopian History: The Case of the Agaw." *Journal of African History,* 29(1):5–18.

Turner, V. 1967. *The Forest of Symbols.* Ithaca, NY: Cornell University Press.

———. 1969. *The Ritual Process: Structure and Anti-Structure.* Chicago: Aldine.

———. 1977. "Symbols in African Ritual." In J. Dolgin et al., eds., *Symbolic Anthropology,* pp. 183–94. New York: Columbia University Press.

Ullendorff, E. 1968. *Ethiopia and the Bible: The Schweich Lectures.* London: Oxford University Press for the British Academy.

———. 1973. *The Ethiopians.* 3rd ed. London: Oxford University Press.

Urbach, E. E. 1988. "Hilchot Avadim Kemakor Lehistoria Hachevratit bimey haBait haSheni ubitkufat haMishna vehaTalmud." *The World of the Sages: Collected Studies,* pp. 179–228. Jerusalem: Magnes Press. (Hebrew)

Wagner, R. 1986. *Symbols That Stand for Themselves.* Chicago: University of Chicago Press.

Waldman, M. 1989. *Beyond the Rivers of Ethiopia: The Jews of Ethiopia and the Jewish People.* Tel Aviv: Ministry of Defence Publications. (Hebrew)

———. 1991. *From Ethiopia to Jerusalem.* Jerusalem: Ministry of Education and Culture. (Hebrew)

Weil, S. 1995. "Collective Designations and Collective Identity Among Ethiopian Jews." *Israel Social Science Research,* 10 (2): 25–40.

Wurmbrand, M. 1971. "Falashas." *Encyclopaedia Judaica,* vol. 6, pp. 1143–1154. Jerusalem: Keter.

Yuval, Israel. Forthcoming. *"Two Nations in Your Womb": Jewish and Christian Mutual Perspectives.* Berkeley: University of California Press.

Zoosmann-Diskin, A., et al. 1991. "Genetic Affinities of Ethiopian Jews." *Israeli Journal of Medical Science,* 27(5): 245–251.

Index

Abba Itzhak *(Qes)*, 22, 49, 62, 128n15
d'Abbadie, A., 128n15
Abel, 38
Abraham (patriarch), 90
ablution ritual, 67, 68, 107–8, 119
Adiaro, 76
Aešcoly, A. Z., 126n7
Agaw (language), 23, 128n15
Agaw, Beta Israel appellation, 21, 80
Agaw-Zagwe dynasty, 21
agreements, land-leasing, 25–28, 108
agriculture, 17–18, 20, 22, 23, 26, 29,
    119; and arrangement linked to arti-
    sanry, 30; labor for, 108; request for
    Sigd prayers benefiting, 60. *See also*
    farming
Ambober (village; Gondar), 53, 57–58,
    61, 86
Amharic, 23, 56
ancestral memory, 74, 78
ancestors, religion coming from, 74
animals: feces canceling impurity, 20,
    119; as gifts to *qes*, 60; sacrificed in
    Beta Israel rites, 62, 63; slaughtered
    by *barya*, 79. *See also* goats, sacrifice
    of; sheep
anti-Jewish accusations, 8, 21, 23, 27,
    35–39, 41, 80, 120, 128n14
appellations: Beta Israel as, 21, 125n2;
    Christian for Beta Israel, 21–23, 36,
    80, 103, 110, 119, 120; referring to
    supernatural powers, 23
Arbatom (Four Fasts), 54
Armacheho, 26

arrangement, linking agriculture and
    artisanry, 30
artisans, artisanship: arrangement linking
    agriculture and, 30; Beta Israel, 29, 32,
    127n6; *buda* associated with, 35, 37;
    supernatural powers attributed to, 7
Asmara, 66
Attinkugn: appellation for Beta Israel,
    128n16; laws, 127n4

baptism, 56, 66, 67, 71, 109, 114, 120,
    121
barya, 73–81, 123
barya Falasha, 76
Beck, Brenda, 105
behavior, as deriving from religious
    culture, 86–87, 93–94
Belesa: attitude towards Beta Israel in,
    62, 127n11; leasing conditions in, 27;
    relations between Jewish smith and
    Christians in, 30; use of term *kayla*
    in, 22
Ben Dor, S., 126n7, 135n4
bet-qeddus, 18
bet-tselot, 18
Beta Christian, 21
Beta Israel, as name, 21, 125n2
Bible. *See* New Testament; Old Testa-
    ment; *Orit;* Torah, fabric covering
billawa (personal knife), 43–44
birth, pure, 103
blessings: before slaughtering meat,
    100–2; for fertility, 62; for rain, 60.
    See also prayer(s)

Text:	10/13 Sabon
Display:	Sabon
Composition:	Integrated Composition Systems, Inc.
Printing and binding:	Edwards Brothers, Inc.